Hearts to Heav

Reginald Frary has sung in his local church choir in Richmond, Surrey for more than half a century and draws on this lifetime's experience in his stories of musical mayhem that have entertained countless readers for almost as long.

This is his fourth volume to be published by the Canterbury Press and follows the deservedly popular *We Sang It Our Way, It'll Be All Wrong on the Night* and *What a Performance*.

Hearts to Heaven and Tempers Raise

Reginald Frary

CANTERBURY
PRESS
Norwich

Text © Reginald Frary 2005

First published in 2005 by the Canterbury Press Norwich
(a publishing imprint of Hymns Ancient & Modern
Limited, a registered charity)
9–17 St Albans Place, London N1 0NX

www.scm-canterburypress.co.uk

British Library Cataloguing in Publication data

A catalogue record for this book is available
from the British Library

ISBN 1-85311-666-1

Typeset by Rowland Phototypesetting Ltd,
Bury St Edmunds, Suffolk
Printed and bound by
Bookmarque, Croydon, Surrey

Contents

'Reg Frary has been entertaining us for some 40 years with his humorous tales of mischievous choristers, vicars and organists, and judging by the number of books we have sold through RSCM, he has many fans.'

Church Music Quarterly

'His stories . . . are told with affection and wit.'

Methodist Recorder

'Frary takes the reader on a journey of brooding musical passions and intrigue . . . that will ring bells with anyone who has experience of a local church or village choir, whether having sung in one or endured the efforts of those who have tried.'

Church of England Newspaper

'. . . whimsical tales to amuse and entertain from a veteran storyteller.'

Christian Marketplace

Preface

In the dear, distant days when I was a choirboy there used to be a tiny cramped shop in a narrow passage off Richmond Green. It was called Noah's Ark and it sold a sturdy variety of workaday men's merchandise from workmen's trousers and heavy duty boots to voluminous, oiled cycling capes, metal tool boxes, scout's knives and lamp wicks. The trousers hung from the boarded ceiling in a circle round the gently purring gas lamp that dispelled the crowded darkness day and night, and the boots marched along the cluttered floor from the shop entrance to the dimness of the back storeroom where shelves of brown paper parcels of workmen's flannel shirts and thick woollen socks reached to the ceiling.

Noah's Ark also sold choirboys' Eton collars. These were the type that needed frequent laundering, but they were being superseded by plastic collars that needed only the occasional wipe with a damp cloth. They were instantly popular – you could wear them for a year or two before they became yellowed and cracked. But they too were consigned to the past by the ruff – the ubiquitous ruff. Now, the Eton collar (with snap-on black bow) was easy to wear and smart. At a stroke it hid frayed cassock tops and protruding scruffy shirt collars, whereas the average ruff, if not scrupulously looked after, rapidly degenerated into the sad form of a bedraggled off-white handkerchief clinging dejectedly around the neck of the wearer.

However, in matters both great and small the church must always be open to change. Survival, we are told, depends on change – even where change proves not to be for the better. But whether church choirs wear collars or ruffs, or no distinguishing apparel at all, whether the church takes away the choir stalls and the pews and herds everyone together on plastic chairs, or whether it's now fashionable to talk of singing songs in church rather than hymns, the tradition of a choir to lead the congregation in Christian worship is a very good one. May it remain and flourish, whatever changes the future may bring.

Reg Frary

1

Attila and the Historical Voice

The other day I received a letter from George the third. I am in touch with a considerable number of correspondents named George and as I have never found it easy to remember surnames I find it very helpful to identify them numerically. George's letters are always full of interest; he only writes to me when there is something sensational to report on the latest crisis in his village church choir where he sings baritone (more or less).

'You don't come across them so much these days,' wrote George, 'but one certainly turned up just as we were finishing Friday night choir practice a month or two ago – a flamboyant character who burst in upon us and said we could call him Ambrose. He was one of those overwhelmingly keen types who suddenly appear in the vestry from nowhere and force the impression on everyone that they have sung with great distinction in just about every cathedral choir and top choral society in the country. Nevertheless they are not too proud to have decided to now devote their precious time to honour *your* humble village church choir by joining immediately and thus by example and inspiration raising the choir's musical standards to cathedral level within weeks!'

As soon as this particular choir practice was finished, and despite the presence of the remarkable stranger (nobody in George's choir takes any notice of interloping strangers, remarkable or otherwise, until they have been around for several months at least), most of the choir moved off smartly to their usual Friday evening 'conference' at The Bunch of Grapes. But before Booksup, the organist, could follow them (he is affectionately known as Booksup because he is always beseeching the choir to 'stand and hold your books up'), Ambrose had insisted on confirming the extraordinary beauty of his voice by treating Booksup to a sample solo that hooted and brayed on and on – and on . . .

Later, when Ambrose had eventually departed, promising to be back bright and early for Sunday morning service, to start the process of raising the choir to supreme musical heights, Booksup joined his choir in the Bunch of Grapes. Only one choir member, a bass, broke off from the prevailing heated sporting discussion to enquire vaguely who was the funny bloke who'd gatecrashed choir practice? Booksup waxed indignant (even more indignant than when the vicar sometimes changed the tune of his favourite hymn to a 'more simple and beautiful modern one' at the last moment before evensong).

'That man's voice must be absolutely unique in this day and age,' he declared. 'The trouble is that our choir, even at full blast, might not be able to drown it out entirely. It's the kind of voice they tried to suppress over a hundred and fifty years ago when they did away with castratos – only it's a lot more piercing and upsetting than castratos must have been.'

'A lot more unprofessional,' offered the bass.

'Yes, that too,' agreed Booksup. 'This Ambrose has resurrected an *historic* kind of voice that should be left buried in history, not be upsetting village choirs in the twenty-first century.'

Booksup reflected again on the solo that had just been so determinedly inflicted on him. 'Come to think of it, it shouldn't be inflicted on *anyone* in *any* century.'

'Sounds it was sort of disconcerting, was it?' suggested the bass.

'That's it,' agreed Booksup, 'sort of disconcerting and outrageous.'

Booksup is an interesting character – a middle-aged, almost always cheerful bachelor whose close companion is a black and white cat, a monstrous moggy called Attila, whose blood-curdling howling terrifies and subdues the dogs for miles around. Booksup, who holds traditional (largely unprintable) organists' views on vicars and church councils, had in his early years embarked on a promising, even brilliant musical career – until it foundered irredeemably when he became involved with George's village church choir. Twenty years ago, on the simultaneous retirement of both the organist and the choirmaster he had agreed to take over both positions temporarily, pending the vicar's and parochial church council's engagement of new staff. Throughout the following decades everybody concerned forgot all about these arrangements and things have just happily muddled along with the 'temporary' man. George says it's all part of the Church's grand old tradition of letting sleeping dogs lie.

Despite Booksup's traditional feelings, however, the choir reckon that, as vicars go, the present man is actually not bad at all. He hardly ever tries to meddle with the music and simply joins in singing the tunes he knows with a very enthusiastic, generally flat sort of growl. There are two basses in the choir who also sing like that so no one complains about the vicar. An ever-optimistic married man with three lively teenaged daughters who never come to church, three boisterous Labradors who insist on coming and a wife who manages them all with a cheerful determination in their chaotic Victorian vicarage, the vicar rejoices in seeing people happy in church. He is unfailingly referred to throughout the parish as 'much loved' because while he finds it impossible to agree with the multiplicity of conflicting views rampant among the choir and congregation, he doesn't actually disagree with any of them. He's always available to those parishioners anxious to tell him how to run the parish and he listens to them with an enthusiastic smile, punctuating the proceedings with 'Good! Splendid! Great! – you are *so* right.' He then passes the whole problem to his warden, an experienced negotiator who smiles a lot and makes everyone feel confident that they have won their point – and everything in the parish carries on in precisely the same way as ever, including the vicar's frequent enthusiastic sermons on wonderful parish togetherness.

Ambrose continued in the choir for some months,

never missing a service or rehearsal and regularly passing hints along the choir stalls in a huge whisper (during the sermon) on how his fellow choristers could rectify their singing errors. The vicar didn't escape this professional assistance. During the hymn-singing he often became very disconcerted because Ambrose would edge close to him and helpfully shriek right into his ear when he sensed that the vicar didn't know the tune and could do with a little help, or thought he *did* know it very well and was bawling away regardless like unto an enraged football hooligan.

Between the pair of them Ambrose and the vicar dominated the singing. True, there was some competition from the choir's only contralto, a large, seemingly ageless lady with corrugated blue hair and no sense of humour who was freshly outraged each Sunday at having her pitch invaded by Ambrose's all-powerful blend of demented barn owl and over-zealous police car siren. The rest of the choir, however, who *did* have a sense of humour, were content to carry on as usual, mouthing and mumbling away, 'doing their thing' unobtrusively while Booksup endeavoured to blend and obliterate everything with splendid Wagnerian organ support.

But then, quite suddenly, the assorted, conflicting views among the congregation began to merge into a single, urgent demand. The choir, being used to all kinds of strange sounds coming from within their number, were indeed putting up with Ambrose very well, but it was a different matter with the congregation. During the family service each Sunday even the welcome (well, to the vicar anyway) happy, homely sounds of the children at the back of the church with skateboards and drums, and the skirmishing of the vicar's fun-loving Labradors, were completely submerged by the historic voice of Ambrose. At an impromptu meeting behind the organ after a family service a number of prominent members of the congregation had their say and all said the same – Ambrose must be stopped. Later, they all went off to see the vicar, who listened to them, beaming as he passed round the tea and biscuits. Then he said how great it was that in this parish everyone could come together in helpful fellowship to discuss church matters and how lovely it was to hear the happy, healthy sounds of children and animals enjoying themselves in church, blending with the thrilling sounds of religious fervour rising from the choir. It was simply great, wonderful, unforgettable – and wasn't Ambrose just *magic*!

The vicar glanced at his watch. Goodness, was that the time? How time flew when one was with friends. Must rush now. Lovely to talk to you all . . .

For some unknown reason Attila, the organist's cat, never went to church. He was well known in The Bunch of Grapes and was a welcome visitor to most of the villagers without dogs, including the village postmistress who felt safe in these dangerous days when he sat hugely on her counter closely scrutinizing the customers with the penetrating eyes of a tiger. But Attila had never been to church. Then, again for some unknown reason, in the midst of the Ambrose skirmish Attila decided one Sunday to accompany Booksup to a family service. He took up a position on the end of the organ stool, purring loudly, and surveying members of the congregation as they moved about the pews selecting positions either from where they could see the preacher in the pulpit or where they would be behind a pillar so that the preacher in the pulpit couldn't see them.

Then, at the last moment, making a scuffling, eager entrance, came the vicar's three Labradors dragging the vicar's wife at an undignified trot. Attila's ears flattened and his purring dropped a tone into a growl. Booksup hissed, 'Not here, you heathen!', the choir processed into the choir stalls and the service began.

It was noticed that for once Ambrose was not in his usual place in the choir stalls and the first hymn, 'Ten Thousand Times Ten Thousand', with its ebullient Dykes tune really went well. During the following prayers the choirman next to George whispered hoarsely, 'Splendid! What a difference Ambrose makes – when he's not here!'

But he rejoiced too soon. Looking hot and dishevelled, Ambrose presently appeared and pushed his way to his place in the choir stalls explaining to all and sundry in a huge whisper that his bike had broken down, and apologizing wordily as he tripped over someone's feet and tipped his bulky A & M hymn book down the back of the blue-haired contralto with no sense of humour. Attila watched, and became increasingly interested in the choir, as indicated by the slashing of his tail in an increasingly vigorous and violent manner.

The climax came when the service reached the spot

where, in the words of the Book of Common Prayer, 'In quires and places where they sing, here followeth the anthem'. The anthem in this case was Sir John Goss's 'The Wilderness', a splendid Victorian anthem that gives all voices a chance to shine. And shine they did, especially Ambrose's. Within seconds the Ambrose sound cut through and dominated all other sounds – until there issued from Attila an urgently, rising, unearthly howl that soon obliterated everything and sent shudders down many spines. Only when it ceased did the congregation realize the choir had reached the end of 'The Wilderness' . . .

Most of the choir appeared quite unaffected by the performance. They were, after all, used to such occasional upsets – these things happened in their choir. But for Ambrose it was different. As soon as he had recovered sufficiently after the service he vowed that he would never – but *never* – forget the nightmare. Never in all the cathedrals in which he had sung so movingly had he ever had such a shocking experience. If he stayed in this choir he would be *completely* overcome every time they reached the spot in the service when the anthem was to be performed – absolutely, *completely* overcome. He was sorry but in the present circumstances there was no way he could continue to lead the choir in attaining cathedral standards.

Ambrose soon identified another village choir on which to bestow his expertise, but this time, before committing himself, he made careful enquiries as to whether any member of the choir or the organist had a church-going cat. Apparently there were some cats about but not one had ever shown any interest in setting a paw inside the village church. The choirmaster did, however, live with a champion Rottweiler and an outsize Irish wolfhound who went with him everywhere.

Ambrose was mightily relieved. He could now go ahead and sort out this village choir. Catless, the good work could go forward and this time he would succeed.

2

As You Were

I had recently returned from a holiday in upper Austria where, as usual, I was constantly delighted by numerous baroque churches, lofty temples, bright and alive within with glorious pastel colours, with altars, pulpits and breathtaking organ cases dripping with gold and silver and all attended regally in paintings and sculpture by winged beings of the heavenly host.

'I think all this kind of thing is over the top,' announced my churchwarden friend James, with whom I was holidaying. 'Far too much flashiness and general glitter, not what I'm used to in our church – not by a long chalk.'

I knew what he meant. James's village church, hidden in a dip in a field behind a barrier of incredibly ancient oaks and surrounded by endless acres of potatoes, presents a very different picture from those of my admired Austrian churches. Inside, the church is a happy, homely place, and it attracts a loyal congregation but no mention in any books on church architecture or historic interest, despite being a listed building. James reckons the tower is fifteenth century, and that it's the only part of the church that has never fallen down or been pulled down and rebuilt in the style of whichever local builder was around at the time. It has a peal of six bells, rung by a team who have never quite mastered the art of ringing (well, never mastered it at all) and fully demonstrate this fact every Sunday. Happily, the congregation are so used to the joyous jangle that most of them think that is how bells are supposed to sound and are very proud of their ringers.

The choir vestry is what is left of an ancient memorial chapel after the installation of the outsized organ in the early nineteenth century. The donor was a musical coal merchant. He was a very big gentleman and did things in a very big way, hence the difficulty in cramming his organ into the small chapel, and the resultant minuscule size of the choir vestry which today is a sort of low passage with choir robes hanging on bent nails on each side.

The congregation fare a little better than the choir spacewise, although James agrees the nave is a rather funny shape. This is due to the efforts of local craftsmen who throughout the eighteenth century knocked holes in the walls and bricked up windows here and there to provide accommodation for the aforesaid chapel, a lumber room for the sexton and a stall for the vicar's horse. There are some very comfortable pews down the centre of the nave and this seating used to be rented. James said it was worth paying – if you didn't, you had to sit in a side aisle furnished only with planks of wood with no backs, set at a sloping angle towards the wall. This was so arranged that if you lost interest in the sermon and fell asleep you toppled sideways, causing a domino effect, and you ended up in a heap of non-paying parishioners on the floor.

James says that on the wall of an ancient side porch, miraculously spared by generations of local builders of the vandal persuasion and no longer used, there is a medieval carving of hell, showing a lot of matchstick-like figures forking a lot of other matchstick-like figures into a furnace. James's great-grandfather used to teach a Sunday school class in the porch and regularly threatened his pupils that unless they behaved impeccably they'd surely end up like the forked matchstick figures. James reckons that in those days they didn't have to endure the racket that they put up with today when the Sunday school joins the family service. He talked with great affection about life in his remote parish and its church in the dip, forgotten by the outside world. He was quietly happy there and hoped things would go on the same for ever.

But even in James's parish the relentlessly probing fingers of progress inevitably reached out and took firm hold. With the advent of a charming, forward-looking lady vicar, an up-to-the minute, go-getting, no-nonsense parochial church council had recently swept into power. Taking advantage of the traditional sluggish or non-existent voting interest of the majority of the congregation, a huge effort – bolstered by the more militant members of the 'Peace in our time' group, the entire church football team and various disgruntled parishioners, who didn't like the choice of Sunday hymns, or wanted to turn the ancient churchyard into a kiddies' playground, or objected to the devil-may-care bell-ringers – had resulted in a solid block vote that had jettisoned almost the entire parochial church council, a monolithic fellowship that had presided supreme throughout the incumbencies of the last three vicars. At the first meeting of the new council, the pressure groups who had combined to produce the successful vote now separated again to promote, vigorously and very loudly, their individual interests and aims. The vicar, a basically peace-loving chairwoman who tried so hard to feel that she was seriously listening to everyone's point of view that she could never work out what her own views were, had a nightmare three hours endeavouring to keep the contestants in some kind of vaguely civilized order, while at the same time calming the secretary who was fighting a losing battle trying desperately to record the chaos in a sanitized form and using quite un-ecclesiastical expletives under her breath . . .

'There'll be big changes once the new PCC sort themselves out,' prophesied James. 'Mind you,' he assured comfortably, 'they can't start mucking about with the actual church – it's a listed building now. Everything has been there for hundreds of years and it's all listed. Everyone in the choir has been there for ages too and I think they must all be listed as well. Nobody has ever tried to change the choir's way of going on. No matter what changes vicars and church councils have tried to make down the years, our choir have remained constant, changeless. They are sort of part of the fabric of the place – them and the death-watch beetle in the belfry.'

James frowned suddenly. 'But come to think of it,

this new lot might just target the choir. Nothing is sacred with people like them.'

'Surely not?' I exclaimed. 'They wouldn't really do that – not *actually* start messing about with the choir.'

His frown deepened. 'I wouldn't bet on it. Vandals who arranged for our church to have plastic flowers all over the place for *harvest festival* because someone is a friend of a friend starting up in the party novelties business and offering plastic flowers at dirt cheap prices – well, I ask you! Such people are capable of anything.'

'Whatever did the vicar say about plastic flowers for harvest?' I asked, intrigued.

'I don't think she noticed they weren't real,' said James. 'I think she always tries not to notice outrageous things anyway. At the service she just beamed at everyone from the pulpit and remarked how lovely and fresh and colourful everything was looking, including the delicious crusty loaf on the altar. One of our choirmen instantly remarked that he reckoned the loaf was plastic too but I think he was just trying to be excessively provocative. He's got a lovely voice so the choir have to put up with him being excessively provocative. And anyway he was wrong about the loaf. Two sparrows had got into the church and were enjoying it right through the service, until the vicar disturbed them by tramping up to the altar to give the blessing.'

In the following months the dominant group in the new church council soon proved to be composed of those members who yearned to pitch the church headlong into the twenty-first century, by turning the church building into a slick community centre with a super gym, indoor swimming pool and arts centre, with a small side room where you could make hot drinks and sandwiches or hold the occasional church service. James said that the choir would not be forgotten – they could lead praise singalongs in the drinks and sandwich room and would be provided with an electronic keyboard once funds had been raised by the sale of the church organ and choir stalls.

Of course, he said, nobody expected this thrilling new thinking to actually be translated into reality. You didn't treat listed buildings like that. The farthest the new PCC would possibly get would be the removal of a few pews, to be replaced with plastic chairs with nowhere to put your hymn book – but the PCC's *ideas* would provide endless interest and foster a resident excitement of enthusiastic support and violent opposition throughout the parish. All in all, the church with its new lady vicar would be presented as alive and kicking and delving and questioning, even to the extent of no one falling asleep during a vital PCC meeting about smiling at each other in church more often, or the vicar's dynamic, PCC-backed ten-minute sermons on increasing the parish giving contribution. In short, the church would have a new progressive vital image.

James continued to keep me in touch with the progress of the crusaders of the reborn PCC. From being a sort of shadowy secret society whose members were sometimes spotted after Sunday morning service whispering together in dim corners of the church or behind the pulpit, the new members now determinedly started taking centre stage in the after-service coffee room, greeting all and sundry with vigorous smiles and handshakes and babbling eagerness to discuss Our Parish – The Thrilling Way Ahead. For those members of the congregation who were not quite quick enough to grab their coffee and escape before the crusaders completely infiltrated the coffee party, the experience could be quite bewildering to say the least, especially if you genuinely tried to concentrate on the crusaders' startling, even revolutionary pronouncements about their plans for the transformation of the parish.

The trouble was, James explained, that each crusader was pushing his or her own personal ideas with such rigid exclusivity that if you found yourself targeted in turn by more than one crusader's view you got such a chaotic impression of what the PCC were actually aiming at, you finally hadn't the faintest idea what anybody was talking about.

So, few in the parish were surprised or in any way disappointed that, after many months of the vital, new-style church council with its enormously enjoyable, lively meetings chattering on well after midnight, tossing around countless irreconcilable personal views and ideas and cheerfully adopting none ('At least I had my say!'), nothing in the church had altered at all. Not a single pew had been removed, not a single plastic chair introduced, no one except the original complainants could be persuaded to sign a petition to curb the bell-ringers, or to rebuke the vicar about her choice of hymns highlighting heavenly choirs singing everlastingly and belligerent Christian soldiers forever charging for the God of battle. But people loved to talk. The new

PCC was good for them and everything in the parish was going well. It now had a vital, twenty-first century image.

But, warned James, that wasn't to say that people shouldn't be vigilant where the PCC were concerned. Members were always poking around the church looking for things to alter. The latest target was the choir vestry. 'Do you know,' he recounted incredulously, 'one of them is actually making a fuss about the nails the choir hang their robes on. He's saying it's essential that they are replaced immediately with proper pegs . . .'

3

A Rough Guide

While I was in that part of the country I absolutely *must* visit the church, the proprietress of my hotel told me. It was a perfect little Norman gem. As the crow flew it wasn't far away, but it was perhaps a wee bit difficult to find. She gave me full instructions and actually put me on the four-hourly bus and asked the driver to let me off at a certain spot. From there, she explained, I could either follow the road or take a short cut which I couldn't help noticing.

Within a few minutes, during which time a kindly passenger completely bewildered me by telling me of at least half-a-dozen alternative routes to the church, the bus dropped me at the appointed spot. This appeared to be nowhere in particular and consisted of limitless soaking wet fields and a small black bull who took no notice of me and seemed to be battering down a five-barred gate.

Now, when walking in rural England, it is always pleasant to get off the diesel-fumed main roads and take a short cut across the fields. These short cuts are marked by carefully concealed or cleverly camouflaged signposts, and generally peter out in a sea of impassable waist-high stinging nettles or at a farm-yard gate decorated with notices saying Keep Out, Private, No Admittance, and Beware of the Dog. In the summer months they are also waterlogged, and watched over by vast squadrons of gnats and great friendly horseflies. Taking short cuts is *part* of a country holiday. It's the adventurous thrill of not knowing where or how you'll end up, or if you'll end up at all, which is so attractive.

In this particular case I had daringly started out along the short cut and had reached the impassable sting-ing nettle stage. As I stood there musing on which direction would inflict least stings, I noticed immedi-ately before me a large portion of an old iron bedstead and a wheel-less twisted bicycle. From under them appeared a stout, filthy-faced urchin of about six. In one hand he held a half-eaten raw carrot and under the other arm a venerable volume of *Encyclopedia Britannica*.

Sometimes if you ask a local inhabitant the way to a local landmark he or she is quite helpful. This inhabi-tant looked very local. I smiled and said hello and could he please tell me the way to the church? He took a contemplative bite of his carrot, pushed the old bed-stead out of his way and said indistinctly, 'We had a jumble sale there last Saturday.'

He dropped the carrot and held out the *Encyclopedia Britannica* proudly. 'My mum got this there. She bought a load of books for 20p, but she only reads murder and love books, so she gave this to me.' I remarked that he was a lucky boy and slowly repeated my question about the whereabouts of the church. The stout urchin picked up the carrot, wiped it down his shirt and signalled me to follow him.

It seemed to take us ages, scrambling through hedges, wading through ditches and, in my case, twisting my ankles in ploughed fields, but so long as I was on the way to the church I wasn't one to complain. After all, I may not have found another living being for miles. I began to feel most fortunate. Abruptly, after negotiating a deeper and tougher-than-usual hedge, we found ourselves in the garden of a single cottage. It was one of those flamboyant, natural wilderness-type gardens, all brambles and corrugated iron and old coppers. For a brief moment, I thought we had come upon the vicarage, but a second look at the cottage changed my mind. It was nowhere near big and barn-like enough and it didn't have any gothic windows or long elegant rusty bell-pulls marked 'Please use the Knocker'.

'Is the church near here?' I asked my guide.

The stout urchin, whose face was by now even more filthy, looked at me with an expression of mingled astonishment and pity. 'Course not!' he said. He waved the remains of his carrot in the direction we had come. 'It's right back there. My mum lives here. I'm just going to tell her I'll be a bit late for tea, taking you to the church. She gets mad if I don't tell her I'm going to be late. Last week I was late when I fell into the river, and she put the jam away. I only got bread and marge.'

A large, red-faced lady appeared at the cottage door brutally wringing out what looked like the remains of a shirt. 'That's Mum,' said the urchin.

She took to me instantly. No matter what her son told her, she was firmly convinced that I had found him wandering and brought him home. She dragged me into the scullery. From under the table on which stood her tin bath of suds she drew out a homely, decaying, suds-soaked velvet armchair and invited me to make myself comfortable. 'Now what about a nice cup of tea?' she asked me as she meted out the same brutal wringing treatment to a pair of red and yellow striped socks generously darned with blue wool.

During the drinking of the tea (conveyed to me in a cracked 'Present from Brighton' mug), the lady told me that she didn't go to church herself because the vicar never came to see her these days, and even in the days when he did come, he always turned up at teatime and expected a full-sized meal. He'd made matters worse by expelling her son from the choir just because, with the perfectly natural high spirits of a healthy lad, he had put a brick through the memorial stained-glass window and left the vestry tap running all night with the plug in the basin. She said the church just didn't under-stand children. It was about time that vicars got up to date and overlooked smashed memorial windows and flooded vestries.

She was, however, quite agreeable to her son showing me the way to the church. She saw us off at the door, wringing out the remains of another shirt all over the floor. 'Yes,' she agreed, in answer to an enthusiastic remark I had made about the great age of the church, 'it's old, all right. Very old-fashioned indeed. That's the trouble, I always say. You can't expect normal healthy young kids to go into those dark, uncomfortable old places. Why don't they pull it down and put up a nice modern building with nice big windows and those tip-up seats like they have at the pictures? What I say is, you can't expect normal healthy young kids . . .'

It was nearly dark when we arrived at the church. A solid downpour of summer rain was well under way. The banging of a heavy door and the grating of a key in a lock drew our attention to an elderly man who was about to leave the porch. He gave me a large happy smile. 'Did you want to look over the church?' he asked. 'Just a bit too late, sir. Open at ten tomorrow.' And he disappeared smartly into the gloom of rain and overgrown gravestones.

The stout urchin looked up at me. I handed him 50p for his trouble. He seemed to take pity. For a moment his expression became thoughtful as he wiped a patch of soap suds from the battered cover of his *Encyclopedia Britannica*. He studied me critically as if trying to divine my literary taste. Then his face lit up.

'Here, you take it,' he encouraged me. 'I bet you could swap it for a jolly good murder or love one at our next jumble sale.'

4

All the Time in the World

The most frustrating thing about public clocks is not so much being unable to find them as finding them and discovering that they aren't going. I know a village full of clocks that don't go.

The school clock has shown half-past three for 21 years. The authorities are going to do something about it as part of the school's forthcoming centenary celebrations. The clock on the village hall is *capable* of going, but they never wind it because it's only got one hand and is considered rather ineffective. The fine clock on the riding stables has fallen backwards into its turret, and the almshouse clock has been struck by lightning. The railway station clock has an out-of-date timetable plastered across its face and there are ugly rumours concerning the reason why *that's* not going.

The Diamond Jubilee commemoration timepiece over the village lock-up is definitely under repair, but there seems to be some difficulty about getting a part for it. Apparently nobody on the parish council quite knows what part is needed or where it can be obtained.

The church clock *does* actually work, but you can only tell the time by it when both hands are on one half of the face, the other half being completely obscured by a delightful pink-flowering weed growing out of the stonework of the tower.

There is a sundial on the front of the Manor House, but no one has ever taken that very seriously.

Now, my wrist seems to encourage watches to go fast, slow or backwards, but never steadily, so on the occasion of my first visit to the village I was as usual not very sure of the hour. I knew it must be almost lunchtime because I felt hungry. Accordingly, I explored the high street and found one of those 'olde English' restaurants with quaint bow-fronted windows displaying little hard rock cakes, big dusty plants and advertisements about Conservative Party whist drives.

Inside, the place was beautifully oak-panelled with a low-beamed ceiling and low oak tables. In fact, the only drawback was that the tables were *so* low that you had to become a first-rate contortionist in order to slide your legs under them without upsetting everything. However, a number of people seemed to have managed it and were grimly and silently eating, as the English do in better-class restaurants.

There appeared to be only one vacant place, a single table and chair crammed under the staircase, and to this a benign elderly waitress beckoned me. The idea was to pull out the chair, crawl into its place, remembering to keep yourself well doubled up so that you didn't crack your skull on the staircase, and then draw the chair in again and gently wriggle onto it. I understand it can be done, but I was, of course, new to the game and not only knocked my head but upset the table as well.

The waitress was most kind and understanding, and waited patiently while I settled in. Then she kindly handed me a large 'arty' looking menu, from which nothing whatsoever was available. But there was a 'special' lunch on, she said, which she could thoroughly recommend. She showed me the details on an atrociously typed postcard – roast beef and choice of two sweets (one of which was crossed out), and tea or coffee. (No reduction if you didn't want the tea *or* the coffee.)

I said I'd chance the 'special', and the first course was soon set before me on a tasteful willow pattern plate – a nicely arranged slice of beef, supported by a splinter of Yorkshire pudding, a baked potato and two sprouts in a little puddle of gravy. All the other diners were still concentrating on eating and the waitress appeared to be at a loose end for few moments, so she started to talk to me. Realizing that I was a stranger she asked me if I liked the village. I said I thought it was priceless.

'But there's always those who are ready to spoil things,' she confided. 'We're all very worried at the moment. There's a dreadful new man on the parish council who actually wants to convert our lovely George IV street lamps from gas to electricity.'

'Why?' I asked, horrified.

'Prejudice!' she hissed and moved away to attend to a man who was calling for the sweet that *wasn't* crossed off.

I quickly took the opportunity to tackle my beef, which was of that variety referred to by a rude friend of mine as the last of the cavalry. Long before I'd made much headway, my waitress was back at my side. To head her off the gas lamps, I asked her what the local church was like, and explained that I hoped to attend a service there on the following Sunday. For a few moments the gas lamps were eclipsed. The church, she assured me, was ever such a nice one and had ever such a nice old vicar, and ever such a nice young organist. There was also ever such a nice verger who ran ever such nice whist drives. She said she went to church quite often. In fact, in the last three months there had been her niece's baby's christening, her nephew's wedding, and old Uncle Charlie's funeral. All the services had been ever so nice . . .

As I dallied with my 'special' sweet – a trifle consisting of a generous chunk of stale jam roll bogged down with bright yellow custard – a tall, jovial-looking young man with a mop of red hair and wearing the most violently multi-coloured hairy sports coat I'd ever seen, entered the restaurant and slid his legs under a reserved table with a skill born of long practice. The waitress, who at that moment arrived with my thimble-full of tea, beamed and introduced him to me as the secretary of the church council. We took to each other immediately and he said it was jolly sporting of me to want to see their church.

After lunch he took me along to the church. We entered first the vicar's vestry, a sort of no-man's-land divided from the chancel by a rusty green curtain. It was a most interesting place for, unlike most vicars' vestries, it contained seven grandfather clocks.

'That's one thing I must mention,' explained the young man. 'We always sing very loudly here. You see, the vicar is an antique-clock collector and these clocks are the overflow from the vicarage. They chime like mad all the time and if we were to sing softly they'd put us right off key, so we have to drown 'em.'

'But they are all showing different times,' I said. 'How do you know which is right?'

'None of 'em's right,' he said. 'We always go by *that one*.' He pointed to a large red tin alarm clock tied to a hat peg on the vestry door. He gazed rather proudly at its vulgar homely bulk. 'I won that ten years ago playing darts at a fair. It's never lost a minute.'

Suddenly the place was filled with a tremendous whirring and clanging. A grandfather clock, which indicated half-past three, majestically struck ten . . .

5

Supporting Cast

The choir of the village church where my Great Aunt Agatha holds sway is the biggest for miles and miles. Every Sunday the flamboyant Victorian choir stalls are overflowing with choir members of all ages, arrayed in superbly tailored cassocks of richest wine red with immaculately laundered linen surplices.

The new vicar is entirely responsible for this splendid turnout. During the first few Sundays of his ministry in the parish, his great sense of occasion was sadly shattered when he found himself conducting services amid the lonely expanse of empty, dusty choir stalls. The last surviving choir member, a venerated figure who as a boy had sung at a service commemorating Queen Victoria's Diamond Jubilee, had recently retired. The vicar immediately set to work employing his considerable charm and powers of persuasion, which included downright barefaced flattery, to recruit an entire new choir, and nowadays, as he never tires of proclaiming, his great joy is to be 'up there in the chancel, backed by my great company of harmonious support'.

The only trouble is that only four people in that great

company can sing or read music, and as for various reasons these singers – a soprano, contralto, tenor and bass – cannot be present together for many services during the year, the choir seldom rises above the limits of a handful of those modern hymns that are presumably intended to be bawled in a sort of football crowd unison and are indeed enthusiastically led by the vicar, who is very keen on football and who, according to the organist, has a sort of modified football hooligan's voice.

Great Aunt Agatha, without whose approval and blessing little can take place in the church, fell instant victim to the vicar's machinations, like almost everyone else in the parish ('I simply cannot believe that you were a land girl forewoman in the Second World War, Agatha. They just didn't allow babes in arms to join the Land Army'), and was one of the first to join the new choir. Within a week or two she had elected herself choir secretary and drawn up a set of rules to be strictly observed by all members. Great Aunt Agatha knowing nothing whatsoever about music and being tone deaf, these rules didn't directly concern music but dealt with items like punctuality, the wearing of suitable footwear to accompany the wine-coloured cassocks (no filthy trainers, rubber boots or high-heeled shoes with sequins), no chewing, whispering or snoring during the sermon, and the absolute necessity for the gentlemen of the choir not to exit from the vestry after Sunday evensong in the manner of a cattle stampede, thus giving the impression that they were trying to beat the gentlemen of the congregation to the pub.

The organist, a competent player, although he much preferred the sound of a brass band going at full blast and, in fact, played first trombone in the local band, had played the organ for so long to empty choir stalls that he completely ignored the presence of the new choir. Indeed, it was generally believed that he didn't even know they were there. He had his own private entrance to the organ loft and, once in his one-man haven, he sat facing his two manuals and became completely engrossed in playing everything in the manner of a giant brass band thundering out a Sousa march. Even during the intervals between the hymns, he was never seen to turn and look down at the choir, but sat seemingly mesmerized by the dozens of photos of steam locomotives that were pinned or stuck over the non-playing parts of the organ. He revered steam locomotives. Between performing in the brass band and on the organ, his great delight was to take turns in driving or stoking an ancient tank engine pulling parties of riotous schoolchildren and older enthusiasts with woolly hats and cameras along a three-mile stretch of line that the railway company had got rid of in the process of 'streamlining the local service'.

Not that the organist was an unfriendly man. Some of the choir members also helped out with the tank engine and had fine times with him in their happy world of steam and nostalgia, but the new choir was never mentioned.

The first time I visited Great Aunt Agatha after the forming of the choir, she invited me to join them for Sunday morning service but warned me not to sing in my normal alto voice because, she said, it wasn't natural and wouldn't fit in and would put everyone off. She said I was to sing the vicar's splendid, relevant, vital, new-age hymns in a manly voice with bags of enthusiasm and spirit, with a smile on my face and joy in my heart. Did I understand? I assured her that I'd got the idea and reckoned I could manage the manly voice all right, but I wasn't so sure about the joyful, heartfelt smile because most earlier encounters I'd had with both the words and music of splendid, relevant, vital, new-age hymns had tended to put me into a very bad temper.

Anyway, on Sunday Great Aunt Agatha took me into the choir vestry and, elbowing her way through a mass of people putting on wine-red cassocks, deposited me with a ruddy, sturdy choirboy with a large round gleeful face, who she directed to brush his awful hair and then to fit me up with a suitable cassock and surplice. The ruddy lad combed his hair back with his fingers and, after the briefest inspection of my person, produced with obvious pride one of the new cassocks, which fitted me perfectly. Adding a snowy white surplice, he asked me if I was used to singing in a choir where I came from, because if I wasn't it didn't matter at all. Take him, for example. He'd never sung in a choir before, in fact he'd never sung at all since he'd been told off about it at school. But the new vicar reckoned you could do anything if you sort of kept on with it. And he was right. 'And now I'm in the choir,' he ended, not without a modest satisfaction.

I said I did sing in a choir and I knew what he meant.

'And how about your organist?' I asked. 'How do you get on with him?'

'Who?' he said.

'Your organist,' I repeated.

'Oh, he's still here,' he confirmed. 'I think he's been here for years and years. But we don't see him much. He's up in the organ loft, you see.' He suddenly beamed. 'Well, we *do* see him. Sometimes he drives this steam train. It's a jolly good train. We all go on it and it blows soot all over people's washing, and they get real mad. It's jolly good fun.'

'I thought he might take choir practice,' I said.

'Choir practice?' he queried. 'We don't have that.'

'No practice?'

'Well,' he amended, 'sometimes just before the service the vicar says he's got another new hymn and he tra-las it to us and then we all tra-la it back, and it goes all right in the service.'

'That's amazing,' I said.

He seemed reluctant to accept the implied compliment. 'Well, not really,' he said. 'All the vicar's new hymns are the same, actually. When you've sung one, you've sung 'em all.'

And as it happened, this was one of those times when the vicar fancied another new hymn. A tall figure, whose middle-aged good looks were enhanced by what Great Aunt Agatha referred to as a 'very classy' silk cassock, he made an impressive entry into the vestry, taking centre stage in front of a huge sepia photograph of a Victorian vicar of the parish who had glared down at everyone for over a hundred years.

The new vicar surveyed his supporting cast with pride.

'Something very special this morning,' he announced. 'We'll enjoy singing *this*.' He distributed to eager hands sheets of pink notepaper on which appeared groups of blurred typed words and, for some reason, a drawing of what looked like a lopsided combine harvester. 'Thanks for the fruits of the earth,' he enlightened. 'Tune written by a friend of mine who does this kind of thing so well. Goes like this.' He thumped the top of the never-used vestry piano and bellowed a cheerful noise for a few seconds, and then we all joined in and tra-la'd when we couldn't read the words, and the vicar said fine, fine, that would be fine, and we all moved into church in a dignified procession while the organist amused himself with some mighty Wagnerian strains from 'The Twilight of the Gods'.

The vicar got on with the service – a colourful mixture of matins, community hymn-singing and whatever came into his head on the spur of the moment – very briskly and I found that I could indeed sing all the hymns straight off as if I'd known them for years. It was only a question of keeping count of the number of times you repeated each line, and there you were. I did at one point repeat a line once too often, but most of the choir did, here and there, and no great harm was done to the overall effect as long as everyone kept on looking joyful.

At the end of the service the vicar paid his usual compliment to the outstanding support of the choir, and we all processed out into the vestry feeling wanted and appreciated. And the man next to me, who was still humming the tune of the last hymn, said there was no doubt about it – a good choir was *most* important for waking up the congregation on Sunday mornings. We left the church together, and as we drew abreast of a small door half-hidden by rampant hollyhocks and two dustbins overflowing with dead flowers behind the vestry, the organist emerged carrying a bulging, battered music case and a shovel.

'He's doing stoking duty on the engine this afternoon,' explained my colleague. 'Why not come along and meet him?'

I too am fascinated by steam power. I eagerly accepted his invitation and later that afternoon found myself among an adoring group of steam buffs gazing at a small gleaming tank engine, lovingly restored, no doubt by devoted weekend workers. Shovelling with a will and a shiny, coal dust-streaked face, the organist was a happy man. During a pause in his labours my choir colleague introduced me. We talked about steam engines, of course, but quite how we later got on to the topic of church choirs I'm not sure.

'I've been thinking of trying to start a choir again in the church,' the organist said. 'We've got some good voices here in the engine shed. We do quite a bit of barbershop singing in our time.'

'But –' I began.

'We really do *need* a choir,' he went on. 'It appears that this new vicar of ours thinks so too. Now and again lately he seems to have even raked up one or two visiting choirs. Goodness knows where he gets 'em from. None of 'em can sing a note – dead useless, all of them, if you ask me.' He wrinkled his brow and took up his shovel again. 'Strange thing about them too – they all seem to wear the same kind of funny red cassocks.'

6

Our Harold

According to my friend Millie, there is always something hilarious going on in her parish, apart from the singing of the choir of which she is a long-serving, enthusiastic soprano member. Over the phone she sounded excited.

'It's this man, y'see,' she explained. 'About 25 years ago he was organist and choirmaster here and we all got on with him like a house on fire. A *really* good bloke was Our Harold. There was nobody who didn't like him and it was a pity he didn't stay with us longer. Trouble was that at choir practice he always instructed us in strictly musical terms – he never shouted things like "Basses, don't bellow like an ox with a hangover," or "Hold your fire in the soft sentimental bits, you insensitive ignoramuses," like our present man does, so no one ever knew what he was talking about. Well, he's going to be in this part of the country for the first time in years and he's coming to choral evensong next month. We want to put on a good show – you know the kind of thing, lots of men thundering away in the back row and a front row packed with attractively gowned ladies and small boys with well-brushed hair and angelic faces. Any chance of you joining us? I thought you might be interested in meeting a choir-master who everyone likes!'

Having eagerly accepted Millie's invitation, I subsequently learned more about the unique choirmaster. At the time of his first appearance at Millie's church Our Harold was a pleasant young man – bright, charming, helpful, enthusiastic and with an infectious sense of humour. But as far as music was concerned he was an outstanding perfectionist. He worked tirelessly with Millie's choir for a full three years before giving up all hope of transforming them from what the vicar's warden referred to as a 'ragtime rabble' into a peerless cathedral choir.

At his farewell evensong service, the choir sang with precisely the same boisterously devil-may-care bravado as they had at his first service, and at the following farewell presentation gathering he still displayed all his endearing qualities and said he'd miss the choir no end, especially the very lively rehearsals they had enjoyed together. He'd really appreciated his time with them. They were the jolliest crowd of companions he'd ever known.

The young Harold had then moved to a neighbouring village church where they had an even jollier choir, and he gave up hope of doing anything with *them* after only two years. For the next two decades Millie followed his progress through a series of village choir appointments where, without exception, the choirs liked him very much and remained musically exactly the same traditional 'ragtime rabble' they'd always been.

Our Harold's stays at successive village churches

became ever shorter and Millie says he eventually gave up on church choirs altogether and formed his own small but very special music society. They dug up ancient music and played it on copies of ancient instruments. The members were all very dedicated, very serious – Our Harold would have welcomed a little jollity but then you can't have everything and he'd found his niche at last.

When Millie and I arrived in the vestry on the Sunday evening of the loved-by-all choirmaster's visit, the present choirmaster was upbraiding a choirboy who was wearing a filthy surplice and a surprised expression.

'But my mum only washed it last week,' the boy protested, 'you can't expect her to wash a surplice *every* day – anyway it's all the dust in this vestry that's the trouble. It shows up on white things.'

'And,' rumbled the choirmaster, 'there's even more dust that shows up on white things behind the bike shed where you lot settle your differences between services on Sunday mornings. When I was a choirboy it was normal to take our surplices off before starting a fight . . .' His beady eye espied another chorister wearing an even filthier surplice. 'And your disgusting surplice is also the victim of vestry dust?' he enquired.

'I dunno,' answered the boy. 'Someone's pinched mine. I found this one at the back of the cassock cupboard – on the floor.'

This present choirmaster has never even dreamed of raising his choir to anywhere near the standard of a cathedral choir or even a respectable village choir. His sole aim has always been to present them in the choir stalls every Sunday in a vaguely civilized state, singing somewhat together and more or less in time so as not to give certain important members of the congregation opportunity to start whinging about them to the tone deaf vicar who thinks the choir are wonderful.

Millie had drummed up a splendid array of volunteers to support the normal choir for the big occasion of Our Harold's visit. A heaving tide of them surrounded Harold as he arrived in the vestry with the vicar who, as usual, was beaming at everyone and vaguely intoning 'Splendid! Wonderful! Jolly good!' Everyone tried to shake hands with Our Harold at the same time and one or two who could shout the loudest got their welcoming words across to him above the wildly enthusiastic uproar that, Millie reckoned, even surpassed 'the shattering racket kicked up by the kids' at the family service each Sunday.

Having experienced the said shattering racket I once asked Millie why such completely undisciplined behaviour was tolerated in church. She said that when long-suffering members of the congregation complained the vicar invariably became very cross and red in the face and said that the sounds thrilled him and gladdened his heart. Millie reckoned that the number of children (with their special noisy toys and super skateboards) was increasing and the vicar was getting more and more thrilled and gladdened – while some of the congregation who seemed incapable of getting thrilled and gladdened had gone off to a neighbouring church where they still had sung matins and everyone kept quiet and behaved themselves and made out they didn't hear it when someone had a coughing fit or dropped a hefty hymn book in the choir stalls and you could actually hear what the vicar was talking about in his sermon.

Having put up with Our Harold's over-the-top welcome for a reasonable time, the present organist, who was feeling rather neglected, bawled to everyone to now shut up so that we could get into the choir stalls and make a start on evensong which was already 20 minutes late. The vicar, faced with his desire to please both past and present organists, continued hovering and smiling at all and sundry and at regular intervals exclaiming 'Good! Splendid! Well, well!' Then he recited the choir's vestry prayer, which none heard, and signalled the crucifer, a retired military-looking man wearing a disapproving expression and a black patch over one eye, to lead on. We all moved at a smart shuffle into the chancel and commenced the service with a spirited rendering of 'Stand up! stand up for Jesus'. We didn't 'stand up' together nor 'raise the royal banner' at precisely the same moment but the resulting sounds were inspiring enough to encourage the congregation to find their places in their hymn books, and quite a few were singing by the time we got to the last verse.

In the choir stalls I found myself next to Our Harold, we being the only two male altos in the choir. Opposite us there rose a forbidding line of contralto ladies who years ago had ousted the choir's ageing male altos and who now didn't seem too pleased to see their kind temporarily resurrected, despite being glad to welcome Our Harold, the legendary very nice choirmaster. He hooted away delightfully, quite oblivious of the darkening looks of the entrenched opposition, but for me it was like being confronted by half a dozen Katishas from *The Mikado* and my voice wavered and slipped off the note far more often than usual.

Truth to tell, I was not sorry when the service was over and everyone, choir and congregation, had gathered in the vicarage to enjoy the official reception for Our Harold organized by the vicar's wife, a famed expert in the generous provision of mountains of tiny sausage rolls and all kinds of tasty morsels on little sticks and gallons of supermarket special offer drinks of all descriptions. A sparkling, beaming lady behind a barrage of bottles called out to me 'red or white' and when I said I'd prefer a cup of tea if possible she passed me on to a hitherto unnoticed large grim-looking lady sitting in a corner beside a veteran tea urn and half a dozen thick china mugs as big as pudding basins. She appeared to be sorting tea bags of all shapes and sizes into separate piles.

'Earl Grey or Ceylon?' she demanded and at that moment I realized that she was one of the contralto barrage that had so affected my singing at the service. I quickly responded 'Ceylon, please,' and she slopped some hot water on to a tea bag in a pudding basin and pushed it towards me.

Meanwhile Millie had appeared at my elbow with Our Harold in tow. She explained me away to him very briefly and Our Harold, after some kindly words about the choir's performance – such enthusiasm, such power (he must have well remembered his myriad, utterly

41

failed attempts at harnessing that enthusiastic power when he was in charge) – was piloted away to meet a bunch of choirgirls, allowing him just enough time to charm them with his well-known fulsome flattery while preventing him from launching into a lengthy criticism in strictly musical terms of their performance of the anthem to confuse them completely.

Late into the very pleasant evening, only Our Harold, the vicar and the choir members remained among the wreckage of the celebration feast. Everyone told each other for the umpteenth time that this was their happiest evening anywhere for years – except for the organist who sat apart at the end of the table, chewing a sandwich and regarding the scene with cynical eye.

At choir practice the following Friday he was, as usual, well on form with his wise words of guidance that all the choir members understood so much more clearly than those mysterious strictly musical terms employed by Our Harold. 'And while I'm about it,' he announced, 'I had a long technical discussion with Harold and I thought you would like me to translate what he said about your evensong performance, so that you could all feel encouraged and happy.'

The choir gathered round him, ready to be encouraged and brimming with proud happiness. He consulted some scribble on the back of a crumpled envelope. 'The overall sound of the choir was shattering in its coarseness,' he read, 'the sopranos were flat throughout and the higher they shrieked the flatter they became, the elephantine sound of the altos needs no further comment, the tenors seemed to be hovering in a nightmare world of their own and the brute force and ignorance of the basses' efforts was truly awesome. Altogether a unique performance that easily overcame the professionalism of the heroic organist.'

The organist put away his crumpled envelope and smiled comfortably. 'Harold said he wouldn't have missed it for the world. And I'll see you lot as usual on Sunday. Don't be late – and see that you're all wearing clean black shoes and intelligent expressions. You know how the vicar worries about those things.'

7

All Things Bright and Beautiful

It was one of those houses where the television set is switched on unceasingly, morning, noon, and night. The family hardly ever watch it, but when a particularly rowdy programme is on and they can't hear each other shouting, someone turns off the sound and leaves the picture flickering and mouthing speechlessly. Regularly, each quarter, the head of the house complains bitterly to the electricity company that the bill is impossibly high and says it's all the fault of nationalization or privatization.

This particular house was the home of a more than usually notorious local chorister, a lad known as Charlie-boy, and the night was choir pay-night at the church. Charlie-boy had been prevented from collecting his ill-gotten gains by a heavy cold, and my friend the organist, who liked to get unpleasant things over with as soon as possible, had brought them to him personally. At his invitation, I had accompanied him.

'They are very nice, friendly people,' he had assured me. 'I can't understand how they could have produced such a fiendish offspring. Unfortunately Charlie-boy is one of our most regular attenders, and I'm on edge the whole time he's anywhere *near* me.'

As we reached the front door, he pulled out Charlie-boy's pay packet. He hammered on the door with a large black knocker, cast in the likeness of a grinning demon's head. 'Fancy,' he mused, 'actually paying for the privilege of enduring Charlie-boy every weekend for six months! Sometimes I wonder why I carry on. There must be easier ways of serving the church.'

The door opened, letting out a blast of TV Western and fried onions. Charlie-boy's mother greeted us with a cheerful shout. 'Well! This is a surprise! Come in, do! Oh yes, thank you, Charlie-boy is *very* much better now. Yes, he certainly *was* sorry to miss evensong. But never mind, I'm sure he'll be ready for practice on Friday night. No need to worry about *that*. Our Charlie-boy is real *keen*!'

She led us to the back room, which we entered by clambering over the family dog. He was one of those large woolly sheepdog types that don't seem to have any eyes or tail. According to my friend, his permanent position was across the doorway, where he meditated deeply and hugged an ancient, mud-encrusted ham bone. Inside the room you couldn't walk more than six inches in any one direction because your way was blocked by elephantine Victorian furniture, designed for a room twice as tall and six times as wide. The congestion problem had been further aggravated by the advent of the television set. A vast mahogany side-board, all scrolls and mirrors, had ended up crushed into a corner with a much fret-worked harmonium, a drunken-looking treadle sewing machine and a battered toy pedal-car. And resplendent in the space so provided stood the television set. It had a large screen – a *very* large screen. It was so large that the only way to focus your vision was to stand half-way down the passage. It rested on a lavishly chromed tubular stand and was surmounted by an outsized china Alsatian dog which Charlie-boy's father had won playing darts at the fair. Charlie-boy's father lowered his newspaper, knocked his pipe out on the drunken treadle machine, and invited us to make ourselves at home and take a seat. There didn't seem to be very many seats, and they were already taken by a collection of people who all smiled at us and carried on knitting, doing football pools and smoking pipes, and stayed firmly where they were. We stood grinning inanely and trying to avoid each other's feet.

On the television screen a tremendous fight appeared to be raging in a Western saloon, where one lot of inebriated gentlemen were firing guns and throwing everything within reach at another lot of inebriated gentlemen, who were also firing guns and throwing all the things back again. At a crucial moment, when someone was about to throw the bar-tender, the scene suddenly changed, and an alluring young lady butted in and started to tell us how she kept her hair so lovely and soft with someone's heavenly shampoo. It was in this brief interlude of gracious living that my friend the organist put on his much-practised hypocritical smile and asked Charlie-boy how he felt. He had just discovered Charlie-boy lying at his feet, eating a jam doughnut, wiping his hands on the lemon-and-pink carpet, and reading a wad of very colourful literature entitled *The Thing from the Black Bog*.

My friend repeated his anxious question three times before Charlie-boy obligingly looked up from the depths of the black bog and said 'Wot?' Then as he saw the pay packet, he lost all interest in bogs and organists' stupid questions. He rose quickly, dropped the remains of his doughnut down the front of my trousers, and expertly grabbed at the packet. My friend produced a small, neatly arranged book in which the choristers had to sign for their pay, and in this Charlie-boy obligingly wrote his name across two pages in a unique tramline style which threatened to cut the paper to ribbons.

Father now lowered his paper again and cleared his throat. He said, 'When I was a boy we had to *work* for our money – a service every day of the week *and* four practices. *And* someone wanting to get married or buried on Saturday afternoon, just when you'd arranged to go to football.' He pointed to a barometer indicating 'much rain'. 'The choir gave me that when I got married,' he announced proudly, 'in recognition of 25 years of faithful service, boy and man.'

He paused for effect, but no one congratulated him, or even said 'Fancy that!' Only Charlie-boy appeared to consider a rejoinder necessary. He stopped counting his pay for a moment and said that a barometer was nothing anyway.

'Everyone in the choir gets one when they're as old as you,' he explained. 'Our top boy says the vicar buys them in bulk at a ridiculously low price.'

My friend the organist, who had started the rumour after presenting the fourteenth barometer in two years, looked suitably outraged and began saying some rather rude things about the top boy, but I couldn't quite catch them all because the TV Western had now returned in all its fury, and a large black-bearded character of the cattle-rustling variety was in the process of being dragged from the local jail and lynched.

At this point, Charlie-boy's mother reappeared on the homely scene carrying a tray of tea. As she expertly negotiated the peaceful sheepdog, the people in the chairs all smiled at us again and cleared the tray of all but one of the cups. Just before I could reach it, my friend took it. Someone passed me the sugar . . .

As we left – reluctantly dragged ourselves away, if you can believe my friend's words to the assembled company – Charlie-boy's mother shrieked across the merry hubbub of the TV lynching party. She assured my friend again that Charlie-boy would be at Friday choir practice.

'He's *keen*,' she said. 'He knows it's no telly or comics otherwise!'

8

Cabbages and Things

I took another opportunity of singing in a different church choir when I visited a relative in a small Suffolk market town a year ago. My relative is himself a member of the choir and is, roughly speaking, a bass.

On our way to matins on Sunday morning he explained that owing to the clergy shortage the parishes of St Mary's and Holy Trinity had recently been merged under one rector, and the choirs of the two churches combined to sing morning services at St Mary's and the evening services at Holy Trinity.

The organist of Holy Trinity was a very advanced and clever young man, and because he was so advanced and clever he realized that any hymn tune that was popular with the congregation must naturally be in the worst possible taste and therefore should be suppressed. Indeed he had told the rector who appointed him that he would never, but *never*, pander to morons who wallowed in debased sentimentality. The organist of St Mary's, on the other hand, *always* pandered to morons who wallowed in debased sentimentality. Consequently the morons, thus splendidly catered for, always sang jubilantly and enthusiastically, and were quite undeterred by the Holy Trinity organist who dismissed their efforts as brute force and ignorance.

On this particular Sunday morning harvest festival was being celebrated at St Mary's, and when we arrived the church was crammed with fruit, vegetables and people. Many of the people were there for the first time since Christmas to make sure that their fruit and vegetables had been placed in the most prominent positions. The whole display was arranged in a highly original manner, and at the back of the church, round the entrance to the choir vestry, it looked as though a laden Covent Garden market lorry had overturned.

Inside the vestry the Holy Trinity organist was suffering. He always suffered on Sunday mornings when he came to St Mary's because he had to take his place in the choir and process up the church through what he shudderingly described as a mass of people bawling their heads off, completely out of tune with the organ, which was out of tune anyway. I was well received, but no one seemed to have heard of an alto before, and I don't think they quite knew what to do with me. Eventually, however, they put me at the top end of one of the choir stalls between the principal soprano and a malformed marrow.

It appeared that everybody in both choirs had made a special effort to be present for the harvest festival, and the St Mary's organist really beamed with pleasure through the bunches of carrots that festooned his console as he watched us crushing ourselves into the stalls and pushing potatoes backwards and forwards along the book-rests to make room for our music.

My recollections of the service can best be described in those classic words, beloved of all who write reports on choir and Sunday school outings for parish magazines – a good time was had by all. Or all but one in this case. We seemed to be continuously singing hymns from huge A & M hymn books that had been presented to the choir by a local post office official and were rubber stamped on almost every page 'St Mary's Church. Not to be taken away.' No one ever trusts church choristers. My relative who sings, roughly speaking, bass, sang it very roughly that morning and, with the rest of us, was most exhilarated with the whole proceedings.

Even the Holy Trinity organist sang the last hymn with a slightly relaxed expression on his face, but, as the principal soprano told me afterwards, that was only because he was looking forward to evensong at his own church, and was happy with the thought that he'd found a new tune for 'Come, ye thankful people, come' which the congregation couldn't possibly sing or even want to sing. The St Mary's organist really excelled himself with the voluntary after the service, and very nearly succeeded in drowning the din from the choir vestry as members disrobed and stood about in each other's way making polite conversation.

From the vestry we joined the main stream of the congregation trying to leave by the main door of the church. Even this presented a problem, however, because some choirmen who were market gardeners were involved in a heated discussion over the rival merits of some particularly bloated cabbages in the porch. It was only when they spotted the St Mary's organist, with whom they had discussed the Sunday morning service at The Three Loggerheads every Sunday for the last 30 years, that they gave over and allowed the flood through.

The principal soprano joined my relative and me, and said she hoped I would be in the choir at Holy Trinity for evensong. She was a delightful girl with a delightful smile, so, readily overlooking the very advanced and very clever young organist who never pandered to morons and who had a new tune for 'Come, ye thankful people, come', I braced myself and assured her I'd face it!

9

Just the Man

Ben and I had lost touch with each other for a year or two when we met by chance, both having been stranded in a London station by the same broken-down train. We are both choristers. He is a back row bass (only does the chorus work) in his village choir. I asked him how things were going at his church.

He appeared most indignant. 'Our organist,' he growled, 'you must remember him – big pompous man with multi-coloured waistcoats and no sense of humour – well, he's suddenly turned into an absolute pain in the neck. He now calls himself the Parish Director of Music because he's in charge of the choir as well as the organ since our old choirmaster retired. Got right above himself, he has – power mad! Well, I ask you,' he boomed, bewildered. 'Fancy him thinking he could get away with *conducting our* choir! We've *never* been conducted. True, we did have that bass who used to beat time by thumping with his boot at the end of the choir stall, but that was different. We've *never* been expected to watch someone waving a stick at us. Now, whenever we sing unaccompanied he says we've got to keep our eyes *clamped* on him all the time. That means we can't even glance at our music and if we don't know the thing we're supposed to be singing we get into the most awful muddle – naturally. Then he starts sighing deeply and raising his eyes to heaven.'

I looked suitably outraged. 'Still,' I sought to console him, 'nobody in the choir could ever read music anyway, could they, so they may as well look at him as at their music if it keeps him in a good mood.'

Ben regarded me sternly, quite beyond my powers of consolation. 'You wouldn't say that if you were at choir practice,' he assured me. 'The trouble is he pulls such awful faces at us while he's waving his stick about – sort of menacing. Murderous in fact – so it's not helpful to the choir, facing murderous looks.'

'I've come across a good few choirmasters like that,' I said. 'He's endeavouring to convey his notions of how the music should sound. He's trying to *enthuse* the choir, to pep them up – or quieten them down if they are bawling out of control.'

'That's no excuse for those demonic faces,' declared Ben. 'Nobody likes him – except the vicar, of course, who thinks it marvellous the way he roars his fiendish great motorbike all over the place at all hours, when he's not pounding on the organ or glaring at the choir. The vicar would like to have a bike like his but his wife won't let him. Every Sunday straight after the family service and matins, there he is closeted with the parish director of music in The Crooked Billet going on and on about bikes for half the afternoon.'

'Funny mixture of interests,' I observed, 'church organs and bikes.'

'Exactly,' Ben agreed. 'You'd never *dream* he was a church organist if you saw him going manic up the high street on his monstrous machine.' He considered for a moment. 'Come to think of it, you'd never dream he was a church organist if you heard him going manic on the organ at evensong.'

'Apart from our director of music's strange new notion that the choir actually needs conducting, what do people think of him and the choir?' I asked.

Ben puckered his brow and sighed. 'Well, the congregation probably don't think much at all. Where the choir and the organist are concerned they *definitely* don't think much at all. They just accept them as a sort of immovable encumbrance that they have to put up with in a brave Christian spirit.'

'Immovable encumbrance!' I echoed.

'Well, yes,' he confirmed. 'Y'see, for the past two years we've had one of those nice modern young vicars here who want everybody to be happy and smiling at each other in church and shaking hands and singing jolly praise songs accompanied by the vicar on his guitar and the vicar's warden on the drums.'

I assumed a sympathetic expression. 'Ah,' I said knowingly.

'But, on the other hand,' explained Ben, 'the vicar has a certain respect for tradition and as the director of music and the choir have little to do with his pop music aspirations and he is a nice understanding man and appreciates their traditional, generous support of church funds, he lets them carry on as the choir and organist have carried on for the last 200 years . . .'

The saga of the choir and the organist who had promoted himself to parish director of music intrigued me greatly so when Ben later invited me to visit him and sing in the choir for evening service I accepted eagerly. The day chosen was Low Sunday – the Sunday when things at the church were getting back to normal after the Easter Day festivities, which in this case had been much enlivened by a huge rumpus involving the choirboys and the Sunday school pupils. Apparently the whole affair had been triggered by an argument about who had found the most Easter eggs hidden in the churchyard by the nice young vicar. Ben said the competition had in fact been won overwhelmingly by the churchyard squirrels, who had followed and minutely observed the vicar as he was secreting the eggs in places in the churchyard known only to him – and to the squirrels, who retrieved most of the eggs well before the human competitors arrived on the scene. The Sunday school team managed to scrape together nearly all the meagre number of remaining eggs and were praised by the vicar as a jolly good team making a jolly good attempt. The choirboys, who were fortunate in retrieving a single egg accidentally dropped among them from an overloaded squirrel store, were condemned by the director of music as being, as usual, as thick as two planks.

Ben and I were early in the choir vestry of his gorgeous fifteenth-century village church. He wanted time to sort out a presentable cassock and surplice for me. Not that anyone in the congregation would notice the quality of what I was wearing, he assured me, because the revered tradition of candle-lit choir stalls was still very much alive here, the only electrical illumination to breach the barrier of tradition being a 60-watt bulb hidden somewhere among the venerable roof beams.

Presently the nice young vicar breezed into the vestry and Ben introduced me. The vicar chortled, 'Jolly good! Splendid!' and slapped me on the back as he went beaming on his way.

Ben then introduced me to the parish director of music who folded his arms across the generous expanse of his puce and gold waistcoat, briefly looked me up and down, instructed Ben, 'He must sit next to you and watch my beat 100 per cent in the anthem,' and rolled majestically onwards. A few minutes later the nice young vicar announced, 'Right, lads and lasses, off we go then', and we all lined up and found ourselves almost running into church to keep pace with the urgent tempo of Johann Strauss's *Radetzky March* which the director of music was pounding out on the long-suffering organ.

The order of service turned out to be something apparently dreamed up by the nice young vicar and consisted of a series of meaningful chats between him and various members of the congregation, punctuated by the frequent singing of praise songs which although enthusiastically performed left much to be desired in the way of singing together and concentration on the same verse at the same time. Then, about half-way through the proceedings, as the strange wild echoes of the singers scuttled away among the roof timbers, the nice young vicar, breathless from his own choral exertions, congratulated everyone on their spirited performance and announced his surprise item for this particular get-together (to sustain interest, each of the nice young vicar's services contained a surprise item). The parish director of music had very kindly agreed to actually *conduct* the congregation in the singing of the rest of the service, thus making the singing even more enjoyable.

Amid a bewildered silence broken only by one strangled voice spluttering, 'Heaven help us!' the director rolled forward to the chancel steps with measured, elephantine tread. He planted his feet firmly centre stage and faced the congregation with what Ben whispered to me was his renowned welcoming expression – a sort of threatening challenge normally reserved for new choir recruits at their first practice. Leaving the choir to their own devices the director of music then proceeded to so flabbergast the congregation with the entire gallery of his fearful faces and excruciating expressions, that at the end of the service the nice young vicar had the hardest task in dissolving the crowd at the back of the church. Instead of everybody shaking hands and congratulating him on his uplifting words and happily strolling off home or to The Crooked Billet, they stood around in enraged or highly amused groups. Whatever was that director man playing at? Had he been trying to do impressions or something, or had the choir upset him? Perhaps he'd crashed his bike. The groups began to converge on the nice young vicar . . .

A few months later Ben sent me a cutting from the local paper headed 'Great success of Superb Demon King'. Apparently one of the many talents of the nice young vicar was writing and producing traditional Christmas pantomimes. This year he'd excelled himself with *Cinderella*, written specially for the parish. The pantomime played to packed houses for a full week in the village hall. The cast, all members of the choir and congregation, were excellent, but the undoubted star of the show was surely the demon king, 'a monster, vigorous, eye-rolling, tooth-gnashing performance thoroughly worthy of the professional stage,' said the report. It went on to identify the actor as a real 'find' – the parish director of music. That gentleman, on being interviewed, admitted to being most puzzled by his choir who had been so persistent, so *determined* that he should play the demon king. 'I have never been in any way drawn to the stage,' he claimed, 'but there you are – talent will out I suppose! Nevertheless I'm still puzzled about my choir . . .'

10

Mrs Go-Forward-Together

The two of us were sitting in the village church vestry surrounded by the glories of the past. At least, according to my friend, that's what we were doing. The main glories as far as I could make out were a row of rusty choir cassocks and fantastically filthy surplices and a large, liberally spotted wall-mirror that made you look as if you had half a face and ears like an elephant's.

And in this venerable atmosphere, as we waited for the church council meeting, at which I was to be an observer, my friend meditated. He said it was funny how you always imagined that your present vicar was the ultimate in hopelessness, yet every time a new one took over he proved even more hopeless. 'Take this parish,' he explained. 'The last vicar was always getting in the way and meddling in things he didn't understand, but the new one is much worse – a most extraordinary character. He thinks he *runs* the parish.'

And it appeared that here he was dreadfully mistaken, for the real power in the parish was a rock-like lady affectionately (or bitterly) known as Mrs Go-Forward-Together. At every church council meeting or garden party she got up and demanded that members of the parish must go forward together. She didn't seem to know where they were supposed to be going, or how far, but the idea was that she ran all the organizations from the church council to the graveyard working party, and always had the last – or only – word on everything.

The former vicar, an elderly disillusioned type, who had long ago done all the going forward he was ever likely to do, had allowed her free rein, and made sure that whoever else's way he got into it wasn't hers. And the other officials were quite content to save time and trouble by agreeing wholeheartedly with her and complaining safely behind her back.

Only the choir had refused to co-operate. The choir never co-operated with anybody, not even the organist. They didn't want to go forward; they were happy as they were. So they ignored the lady, and she in turn didn't like them at all.

But now the vicar was putting up a fight for leadership. He was young and determined, and he dealt very firmly with Mrs Go-Forward-Together. He was also very musical and seemed to have great difficulty in warding off a fit every time the choir sang. My friend felt that this was hardly the right attitude to take. It was true, of course, that not all the members of the choir could read music or pitch a note, but the two who could had always been very democratic and never held themselves aloof. The feeling was that the vicar should follow their example.

Regrettably the vicar was following no one. He was out in front leading. And out there with him – leading in the other direction – was Mrs Go-Forward-Together.

At this point in my friend's story of the village-shattering struggle for power, the church council arrived in two station wagons, so he sat me at the back of the vestry on an ancient wicker laundry basket. The basket was a little uncomfortable owing to a number of broken ends of wood which kept digging into my legs, and I had to hold myself very upright, because if I relaxed the handle of the safe door dug into my back. The evening was somewhat chilly and to add to my comfort someone passed me an oil stove, which promptly started sending up fascinating little wisps of black smoke and surrounding me with a homely odour of paraffin oil.

So intrigued was I by the stove that some minutes elapsed before I realized that the meeting was now in full swing. A man in the back row, who wouldn't speak up, was complaining to the vicar about the acoustics of the church, the length of the sermons and the draught under the west door, and the vicar, who couldn't hear a word, was trying to look interested. Finally, he smiled vigorously, and said he thought it was a very good suggestion, and he would ponder it.

Then, just as the organist discreetly completed a very good sketch of the vicar's warden, who was already asleep, the vicar dropped his bombshell. He spoke firmly and triumphantly, as befitted one who had managed to raise a major issue a fraction of a second before Mrs Go-Forward-Together could sound her famous battle cry and take over the meeting. He said that he understood the usual practice was to take the choirboys on an annual outing to the neighbouring zoo. But in the light of the choir's musical standard, he felt strongly that the money could be spent in a way far more beneficial to the boys. He was on the point of fixing up a weekend voice-training course. He wanted the council's approval right away.

There was a stir in the council. There was a vague suspicion that things were going wrong. By now, members should have been comfortably settled down, while Mrs Go-Forward-Together took up the rest of the evening with her stirring call to action. But whatever was the vicar up to now? The boys had *always* been taken to the zoo, and their fathers before them. Everyone knew the zoo. It was small and exclusive, and consisted of a help-yourself snack bar, a kiddies' model railway, a venerable moth-eaten lion, and a retired coal horse. They all remembered rides on the coal horse ...

And then, rock-like and reassuring, Mrs Go-Forward-Together rose to wind up for the opposition. She said that a beloved tradition, a way of life, was being threatened with extinction. The church council must not countenance such a suggestion for a single moment. The council and the choir must go forward together.

The tension eased. Members relaxed with relief. Everything was going to be all right.

The lady won the day. The choirboys went to the zoo. But I heard later that the choir were in a very awkward dilemma. On the strength of their temporary alliance, Mrs Go-Forward-Together and the choir had become almost friendly, and the lady had invited herself into the choir. Now she runs that, too.

11

Jeremiah Tomkins

Nobody really knows why my cousin Harry's cat is called Jeremiah Tomkins. There have always been cats in Harry's family and they've always been called Jeremiah Tomkins. There is a story that somewhere around the middle of the nineteenth century there was a wayward daughter who gave up attending the local Church of England church with her family and joined the Methodist church, to which she was drawn by an attractive young minister named Jeremiah Tomkins, and that the first cat called Jeremiah Tomkins was named after him. Harry, however, says this is only a scurrilous rumour put about by an enraged grandfather who couldn't bear the thought of a member of his family going to perdition with the Methodists and who simply hated cats.

The truth may never be known, but there is no doubt that the present-day Jeremiah Tomkins is a worthy successor to such a long line of forebears – a shaggy rusty black, a mighty hunter and fighter, an unbeaten defender of a wide territory around Harry's house, a battered, cheerful, clever feline much admired by Harry and his wife and properly respected by the family Alsatian.

And on this particular evening Jeremiah Tomkins and his kind were very much in my mind. I was taking part in a committee meeting to plan the first ever animal thanksgiving service to be held in the village church where Harry is organist and choirmaster. The committee was composed almost entirely of choir members. All the committees in Harry's parish are composed almost entirely of choir members because the choir are the only efficient organization in the parish and generally run the whole place. I had been invited to join this committee because I'd been involved elsewhere in animal services, and anyway I always sang in the choir on my not infrequent visits to Harry.

The single non-choir member, apart from the vicar, who acted as chairman, was the Committee Lady – an elderly wispy character who is always darting about the church with the speed and uncertainty of direction of a dragonfly, with her arms full of flower vases, parish magazines, forgotten umbrellas and scarves and wildly wriggling infants who think the family communion service is a funfair. Like the choir members, she serves on every committee in the parish. Her speciality is to arrive half an hour late for a meeting, request an immediate recapitulation of what she has missed, and then hold the floor for another half-hour to explain why the rest of the committee should think exactly as she does.

The vicar, as chairman, said very little. A tall, vague, puzzled-looking bachelor of uncertain age, with a row of vintage car club badges pinned across his cassock, he is one of those clerics who dismiss the animal kingdom as a baffling eccentricity of the Creator, and any regard

65

or concern for that kingdom by humans as an even more baffling eccentricity. In fact his only previous connection with animals in the parish was the erection of a No Dogs warning in the churchyard. But he is an incurable innovator of boundless optimism and, having tried to fill the church with motorbike services – 'Your motorbike is welcome' – and poetry readings and religious panel games in place of choral evensong, with scant success, he was quite willing to see what the animals could do. He smiled encouragingly at the committee and kept on eating salted peanuts from a little earthenware bowl marked CAT.

We were well into the second hour of the meeting and the Committee Lady, having delivered herself of her usual half-hour directive, which included a demand that on the day of the service all the kneelers should be removed from the pews and the mats from the church porch in case of 'doggie accidents', had taken out her knitting and left us to manage as best we could. Various suggestions had been put forward, puzzled over and gently dropped, and then our bass soloist solemnly knocked out his pipe on the sculpted head of an eighteenth-century vicar that glared at him in a most disapproving manner, and asked, 'What about the music? What do you sing for animals? I once had a ferret who used to go berserk when I whistled "O perfect love". We'll have to be careful about the music.'

I suggested that about the only hymn that our hymn book seemed to offer in that line was 'All things bright and beautiful'. The vicar turned up the hymn and looked at it as if he'd never seen it before – and this may have been a fact, for this vicar, a rigid devotee of modern hymnology, never sang a Victorian hymn and during the singing of such (Harry chose the hymns) would stand absently watching the chancel ceiling and twirling the tassel of his cassock girdle faster and faster.

Harry, after some thought, stepped into the breach and said that 'bright and beautiful' really only half applied to Jeremiah Tomkins. He was bright all right – he could probably talk if he cared to – but as far as beautiful was concerned, he'd never be that, with his moth-eaten coat and shredded ears. A member of the choir who worked at the local brewery said it was the exact opposite with the brewery's new one-and-a-quarter ton Shire horse, Bomber. Bomber certainly had a sort of massive beauty, no doubt about that, but he was so stupid that he could lose his way walking across the stable yard.

The vicar, who doubtless felt that by this time some contribution was due from him, now proposed that we should settle for 'All things bright and beautiful' as the opening hymn of the service – and had anyone got any suggestion for further, preferably more modern, meaningful hymns? A contralto lady who was very poetically minded and had once had some verses about walking along a canal bank in the pouring rain published in the local paper (she'd had dozens of copies made, many of which were still stuck all over the vestry) coyly suggested that she should write one or two animal hymns about which she already had some simply heavenly ideas.

After a short meditation on this, the committee

grunted its usual relieved approval when faced with awkward situations for which they could think of no other solution, and our bass soloist suggested that the final hymn should be 'Fight the good fight' because this was the favourite hymn of his granny who kept three dogs, two cats, a snake and a canary and loved all animals.

A week or two later, when I arrived at the church for the animal thanksgiving service, the bass soloist's Boxer dog gave me his usual enthusiastic welcome, pitching me headlong into the vestry where the choir and their pets were joyously assembling. Dogs of all shapes and sizes (mostly very large) were straining at leashes trying to establish contact with a number of cats who regarded them loftily from baskets and cardboard boxes with holes in them. Someone had put a frog in a plastic box on the piano, and a rabbit and a budgerigar studied each other quizzically from their respective containers on the vicar's desk. The vicar plodded about looking utterly bewildered and, coming up to Jeremiah Tomkins, assumed the tone he always used (quite unsuccessfully) when trying to charm bawling babies in the church crèche. 'Hello, pretty Tiddles,' he crooned, poking his finger into Jeremiah Tomkins' basket. Jeremiah, recognizing a fake, promptly nipped him.

In fact Jeremiah Tomkins had had the vicar summed up within hours of his arrival in the parish. Jeremiah was an old hand at coming to church. Living next door to the church, he had staked his claim to the territory long before the advent of the present incumbent, and each Sunday at matins took up his position on Harry's organ stool from where he regarded the vicar with an unblinking stare throughout the service. At first the vicar found this rather disconcerting, but after a time learned to resist the futile temptation of trying to out-stare Jeremiah Tomkins.

And so the first-ever animal thanksgiving service at Harry's church took place and was a great success. The vicar sat amid the huge congregation of man and beast and wondered, amazed, why so many people came to a service like this when only half-a-dozen or so turned up for his motorbike services and poetry readings and religious panel games. He didn't understand it at all but he did understand that the church was full. He felt almost elated as he stood at the church door after the service. Not only did he have an appreciative word for every human, he acknowledged the animals, at least the dogs and cats. In his crèche voice he addressed each dog as ' – er, Dog' and each cat as 'Tiddles'.

A few days after the service, Harry and I went to lunch at the vicarage. As the vicar greeted us, a small knowing-looking tabby cat skittered around his feet chasing a ball of paper. The vicar noticed our looks of amazement. 'It was left over from the animal service,' he explained. 'It appears to have come on its own. It seems to have adopted me.' He smiled in a puzzled manner. 'The vicarage cat,' he pondered. 'I wonder if he'll come to church like – er – your cat, Harry?'

'What's its name?' I asked, intrigued.

The vicar seemed slightly surprised by my question. 'Tiddles, I suppose,' he said.

12

The Older They Get

You can generally tell what kind of set-up they have in a country church as soon as you see the church-yard. If the gravestones have been uprooted and stood round the walls like soldiers, and someone has planted a goldfish pond right in the middle of the resulting open space, then you can be pretty certain they've got a progressive vicar and church council. If, on the other hand, the lych-gate falls off its hinges as soon as you try to enter the churchyard and you can't see the path for creeper and bits of broken gravestone it doesn't necessarily mean that things are dead. It's more likely that those in charge are fascinated by rustic charm and don't want to change things or squander any money. You will doubtless find that the vicar is still in the nineteenth century, and indeed has probably been the vicar ever since the nineteenth century.

The church I found in the wilds of Hampshire one Sunday morning was definitely of the latter kind. The lych-gate didn't exactly fall off its hinges. I had to lift it off because the latch was firmly padlocked. Fighting my way through the undergrowth I soon discovered that I was not alone. A large number of choir-boys were sitting around, half-hidden among the memorials, listening to a lad with red hair who was speaking from the top of the Manor House family vault. I didn't want to butt in on what was obviously an important meeting, so I asked one of the least dangerous looking choristers on the fringe of the crowd where I could find the vicar or the organist. He explained politely that he couldn't help me because all the choirboys were on strike. They'd just formed a union and were demanding their rights.

At that moment, however, the organist arrived and broke the strike. He was obviously a man who didn't believe in unions or rights because he achieved his results simply by clouting the red-headed speaker with a manual of organ voluntaries and driving the whole mob into the vestry.

As is my custom, I introduced myself, and got invited into the choir for matins. The organist, a veteran of the old school, explained about the choir. He said the boys weren't a bad lot really. There were a few broken windows from time to time of course, and one of the organ pipes had recently disappeared. 'But it's the *men* who are the trouble here,' he complained. 'They lead the boys *on* so. I can never do anything with the boys while they are in the same vestry as the men.'

So the men had now been segregated in the tower room above the vestry, and the boys were almost manageable. The organist showed me the spiral staircase leading to the tower room. 'Go right up,' he invited. 'Someone will find you some things to wear. I believe the old verger's cassock is still there. No one has worn it since he died, and he was just about your size.'

At the top of the stairs I entered a cell-like cavern full of brown photographs of Victorian vicars and the smell of boot polish. A dozen or so men in stockinged feet were padding round an enormous refectory table on which stood a vase of dead chrysanthemums and a mass of muddy boots. I again introduced myself, and one man who was attempting the clean the boots offered me the only chair in the place. He was most friendly, and before I'd had time to remove some more boots and a pile of dirt from the chair he was well into his story.

Apparently the traditional way for the choir to approach the vestry (and most choirs *are* traditional in their approach, despite new vicars who always want to alter everything) was through an alley known as Lovers' Lane, which was always full of mud and broken bottles. It was possible to avoid the broken bottles but not the mud, thus the ceremony of the boot polishing always preceded a service. Being unacquainted with this particular Lovers' Lane my shoes were reasonably clean and I felt very much out of things. Indeed, I became positively uneasy when I noticed one the Victorian vicars glaring at me from his brown photograph. He had the Mona Lisa quality about his eyes and wherever I moved he still kept glaring at me . . .

However, the late verger's cassock fitted me very well and I was as presentable as the rest when the senior choirboy gave a piercing whistle up the stairs and informed us the 'Old Man' was ready. It was obvious that the vicar was happy in his work. Large and round, he stood among us smiling hugely, a delightful ancient cherub. Then, at a lift of his finger the talking ceased and the shining boots of the choir plodded sedately from the vestry to the chancel. Our entire way lay across large iron floor grids through which was supposed to issue warm air to heat the church. Something must have gone wrong down below, however, because liberal gusts of sulphurous coke fumes were choking everyone for yards around.

But it's possible to get used to anything in time, and it didn't take us long to get into our stride with the first hymn. You could aptly describe the sound as a loud jolly noise, but the tune was based on one of those German chorales that never seem to know when to stop, and I must confess my attention wandered a little. It was finally held by an epitaph on a stone slab at my feet. This was all about a gentleman who had managed to live to 102, and then been foolish enough to get run over by a steam engine. The psalms and canticles were sung to chants I'd never heard of, from books that were out of print. Only two men appeared to have copies, and they never opened them. That, of course, is the advantage of singing the same chants every Sunday for 50 years.

But we kept coming back to the German chorales. The lessons and sermon were short, but the chorales roared on and on, and by the end of the service I had read two dozen more epitaphs.

When we had returned to the tower room some choirmen offered to show me the quick cut through

Lovers' Lane, but I was wearing only low shoes so I regretfully declined. As I left the church by the lych-gate the strains of the organ voluntary followed me. I recognized another German chorale.

13

O Perfect Love

Parish councils often get blamed for doing nothing, and this is rather a pity. Generally, if they *do* attempt something, it causes so much trouble and upsets so many people for so long that it's far better for nobody to do anything.

In the particular village I have in mind, the parish council had recently replaced the gas street-lamps with electric ones, and this meant that the village's Very Superior Lady, who always got served first in the local shops and completely monopolized the vicar in the church porch after Sunday evensong, now had to switch on her bedroom light when she prepared to retire for the night. Before the parish council had started interfering, she had never used the bedroom light because a gas lamp outside shone right into the window. But now they had taken it away and erected a new electric standard farther down the road, outside a defunct fishmonger's shop that didn't have a bedroom anyway. People just couldn't leave well alone . . .

And it is the same with church councils. Still in the same village, there was the case of the parish horsetrough. It belonged to the church, and was let into the graveyard wall which bordered the village street. It was a venerable and elephantine piece of work, and had been used by generations of horses who drank from it on their way to and from the market, and by generations of choirboys who threw each other into it on their way to and from the church.

But now only one horse – a greengrocer's – remained, and the church council, having nothing particular to argue about and hold over until the next meeting, felt that the trough had outlived its usefulness, and no longer warranted its prominent position. Someone had an idea about replacing it with a nice concrete seat (concrete was so much better because it never needed painting) backed by a large, gaily-coloured, floodlit noticeboard and neon sign, which could not fail to attract attention to the medieval church. Few councillors considered the claims of the lone horse, and no one at all thought of the choirboys.

For weeks now, various councillors had stood around, gazing at the trough and making notes, as if it had suddenly appeared from another planet. The local paper had devoted half its front page to a quite unrecognizable photo of it (as seen from the William the Fourth) and a man from the local historical society had measured it up 17 times. Only with the greatest difficulty could the greengrocer's horse even approach it.

And talk of seats had raised another matter in the church council – the question of removing the back pews in the church. In a rather unfortunate speech the vicar had said that, during the last 50 years, as the number of carthorses using the trough had regrettably decreased, so had the numbers of the congregation using the pews. He didn't seem to appreciate the verger's difficulty in deciding where he could put all the disused flower-pots, worn-out hassocks and discarded hymn books that had been stored in the back pews for years, and when someone said that it might be difficult to obtain a faculty for carrying out the work, the vicar confidently waved the fear aside. They had the backing of the bishop, he explained. The bishop was a very progressive man and revelled in removing things.

As I entered the tiny church on a brief visit one weekday afternoon, I heard the huge voice, and recognized the commanding presence of the Very Superior Lady who had been so badly treated by the removal of the gas lamp. She had apparently borne down on two harmless middle-aged ladies who had just wandered into the church to look around. She towered over them, looking remarkably like Tenniel's conception of the Duchess in *Alice in Wonderland*.

'We haven't got any brasses here,' she was declaiming, 'but we've got some absolutely *splendid* memorials.' She pointed to a very large marble contrivance that defaced most of one wall. 'My great-grandfather – Captain, Indian Mutiny, y'know.' She pointed to an even larger contrivance that did the same thing for the opposite wall. 'Great-uncle – Major-General, South African War – High Sheriff of the County – very respected church-man. Got three organists dismissed for incompetence – always hated the choir. Wonderful man!'

The two middle-aged visitors cowered together and twittered, 'Very nice – very nice indeed.' Then, to their great relief, the Very Superior Lady spotted me. Despite my efforts, she knew me slightly from previous visits, and always liked to corner me for an hour or two. She dismissed her audience, who thankfully scuttled away, and sailed up to me with outstretched hand. She regarded me with an expression of mingled pity and contempt. She took a deep breath.

'And how's the world treating you?' she bellowed. 'You don't look very well. Never do! Always seem to be feeling the *cold*! Good heavens, it isn't cold *today*! Have you heard about this disgraceful business of the horse-trough and the pews?'

Quickly I interjected, 'Yes.' I knew I'd have no time to say more.

She thundered on. 'Of course, it's not really the vicar's fault. Type that's so easily *led*. It's the new curate. Very self-opinionated. Comes here from some unheard-of place and starts *agitating* straight away.'

According to her account, the new curate hadn't liked horses since the day he'd been thrown by one, head first, into the choirboys' sandcastle on the annual choir outing. The whole choir had seen him. And as for the pews, he seemed to have a sort of mania about them. At every church where he'd served he'd left a trail of removed pews and furious vergers with homeless lumber.

The lady paused for a brief moment to glare down the church at a scarecrow figure who had just entered and was loping up the aisle. This was the organist. 'Not a bad musician, I suppose,' she grated, in what she obviously imagined to be a discreet whisper, 'but hopeless with the boys. No control whatsoever. My great-grandfather would not have tolerated him for a moment.' Her voice echoed in every corner of the building.

As the organist came up to us she dropped her whisper and addressed him in her usual shattering tones. 'I was telling Mr – er – what the church council are trying to do to our church.'

The organist came out of a deep reverie, pushed back his mop of grey hair, and seemed to mumble more to himself than to us, 'Spending pounds and *pounds* on pulling out horse-troughs and pews, and here we are with mould in the organ. It's so damp it's growing mould. Fancy! Mould in the organ and they're worrying about horse-troughs and pews!' He loped on his way and disappeared up some stairs into the gloom of the mouldy organ.

On a December afternoon some months later, I had occasion to visit the church again. Surprisingly – or was it so surprising? – the horse-trough was still there and the back pews remained in their places. Up by the chancel screen the organist and the verger were gazing morosely at a mass of dismantled organ pipes strewn all over the front pews.

'Well,' I greeted them cheerfully, 'you haven't lost the horse-trough or the pews after all.'

The verger raised his head dejectedly, and explained briefly the situation. It seemed that some unscrupulous estate agent had at last succeeded in selling the derelict Manor House to a lady who was going to use it as a very exclusive boarding school for girls. The Sunday morning church congregation was therefore likely to be doubled, and all the pews would be needed. Also, one of the school's most carefully nurtured accomplishments was to be horse-riding, and a number of horses would be daily passing the church. So the trough was reprieved.

'Fine,' I enthused. 'So everything's all right now. And I see that the church council are spending the money on the organ.'

'All right?' repeated the organist, incredulously. 'All right! Taking my organ to bits just before Christmas! How do you think I'm going to get through all the Christmas music? Sabotage, that's what it is!'

And the verger was equally offended at my unfeeling remark. 'Selling the Manor House, indeed.' His voice quavered with indignation. 'Just think of it' – and it was evident that he could hardly bring himself to do so – 'hordes of kids crowding the pews. Where do you think I'm going to put all my flower-pots and hassocks and hymn books? I've got *tons* of stuff down there!'

Yes, there's no doubt about it. It's often far better for nobody to do anything!

14

Semi-United We Stand

One of my village church organist friends, Hacksaw (of whom I have written on a number of occasions), still holds together and rejoices greatly in his choir, who are regarded in the parish variously as a superb, inspired band of singers, a rowdy rabble lacking all musical sensitivity, but jolly good for a massive carol bawl at Christmas, or simply a recurring, unmitigated disaster. Needless to say, the first view is held exclusively by Hacksaw and the members of the choir, and the alternatives by members of the congregation and any casual visitors who may have unsuspectingly dropped in for evensong. Hacksaw says that if the vicar has a view on the choir it is a secret one because he's always preaching on Christian co-operation in the parish, which excludes having nasty thoughts about anyone, even the choir, and he's tone deaf anyway.

For generations the choir vestry has been accommodated in a small, irregular, cobwebbed area behind a venerable green curtain at the back of the church. However, for some time now it has been very obvious, even to the church council, that the place has become quite unsuitable for the increasing number of ladies who have been attracted to the choir, or to Hacksaw, who with his flamboyant showmanship style on the organ, his intimate smiles, fulsome compliments and elegant attire is really quite an attractive bachelor despite his advanced years. So, recently it was decided that the ladies of the choir should take over the choir vestry, which was to be thoroughly cleaned from the grime of ages, and the single cracked mirror and leaking hand-basin replaced with all the modern paraphernalia deemed necessary for presenting the ladies in the choir stalls each Sunday in the most aesthetically pleasing manner.

A new place has been found for the choirmen. When the verger had been prevailed upon to tidy up his 'glory hole', a twilight zone for lumber behind the organ, and remove a defunct lawnmower, several battered buckets, two or three mops that had seen their best days and a broken stepladder, it was surprising how much room there was for the men to robe. And the discovery of a small boarded-up door giving access to the churchyard was an unexpected bonus. Opened up, it offered the opportunity for the choirmen to unobtrusively slip outside for a quiet smoke during the sermon.

For the first few weeks after the rearrangement of the choir accommodation, all went well. The ladies' vestry, having been speedily redecorated, became a place of delicate colour and light, its new attraction enhanced by tasteful miniature vases of flowers perched before the sparkling tinted glass windows that formally had shed only a sombre glimmer through layers of dusty dark ivy.

The choirmen's new abode remained much as it had always been as the glory hole, especially after the verger had edged back the lawnmower, buckets, mops and the broken stepladder because he could find nowhere else to park them. Hacksaw said there must have been more daylight in the place years ago when there was no organ and the choir sat in the gallery at the back of the church accompanied by a man who played a cello so badly that no one could tell whether the choir were singing sharp or flat or not singing at all. No one ever complained, however; the man was much revered by the choir and organist because he always provided the most lavish annual choir dinner and it was rumoured that his great-great-great-uncle had once actually had a word with Mozart.

Eventually, however, a well-off neighbouring farmer who was a good friend of the vicar's because the vicar let his pigs wander all over the churchyard, endowed the church with a very large pipe organ to commemorate Queen Victoria's Golden Jubilee. The monster took up half the verger's glory hole and completely blocked out the only window. It was a pity about the lack of light thereafter, but of course musically the great improvement was that the choir had no more use for the demon cello player who, local history has it, went off in a huff and joined the village chapel. Things weren't so good for him there, however, because almost the whole of the service time was invariably taken up with blazing hell-fire sermons and there was not much room for music. However, he did have a regular spot when he played his cello immediately after the sermon while the congregation meditated on what they'd been threatened with.

But, back to the present at Hacksaw's village church, the choir were still amicably divided, with the ladies and children in their tastefully renovated vestry at the back of the church and the men firmly installed in their haunt behind the organ at the other end of the church. Of course, all the members appeared together when singing at the services, the men trekking down to the ladies' vestry at the last moment to process up the aisle to the chancel in a show of choral solidarity.

To further support the impression of a united organization, the tastefully renovated vestry occupants and the glory hole denizens came together for choir practice each Friday evening and life in the choir jogged along quite happily – quite happily, that is, until the enthusiastically heralded (by some anyway) arrival of the parish's first ever lady curate.

'She's quite young,' Hacksaw explained to me over the phone, 'and apparently she's one of those "loving togetherness" people – you know, she wants everyone in a huddle in the centre of church. She doesn't like choirs sitting on their own up in the chancel and she won't go up into a pulpit to preach. She says she wants to be among the people chatting with them, not looking down on them preaching at them.'

On her first Sunday on duty the new lady curate had arrived bright and early at the church on her mauve motor scooter, before most of the congregation and choir had arrived. She looking in beamingly at what she thought was the choir vestry (no one had yet enlightened her that this was dedicated strictly to the use of the lady choristers) and spotted a lone member who was arranging fresh flowers in a cut glass vase. 'Hi,' greeted the new curate. Her eyes travelled from the flowers and over the tasteful sunlit surroundings. 'How lovely,' she enthused. 'Absolutely unlike any other choir vestry I've seen.'

The young choirlady looked up from her flowers, matching the curate's beaming smile. She it was who was secretly known by her colleagues as the belle of the ball because, although she couldn't sing in tune for more than a few seconds together and never seemed able to find the next hymn in time, she was a most attractive looking girl and, as the organist said, 'charming with it' and looked good in the front row of the choir stalls. She said, 'Well, it's the absence of men, you see – the reason why this is such a nice looking vestry, I mean.'

The new lady curate's smile became puzzled. 'But you have men in the choir?' she queried. 'I think the vicar told me . . .'

'They're behind the organ,' explained the decorative soprano. 'It's a sort of lumber room with no windows where they can be as untidy as they like and smoke and talk about football and horses all the time. My Uncle Fred is one of them. He sings bass and he's always organizing trips for the choirmen to big matches and breweries. We don't have much to do with them except in the choir stalls. They're all old like my Uncle Fred and our organist is one of them – ever so keen on big matches and breweries he is.' The decorative soprano smiled enthusiastically. 'The choirladies like him, though,' she said. 'He's always so very charming to us and always congratulates us on managing to get through the services without breaking down.'

When the new young lady curate fully realized the choir vestry situation she was at first shocked and then became very sad at the lack of togetherness in the choir. In various ways she went ahead, coaxing the other usual warring parish groups into a more or less non-belligerent whole with a sense of Christian unity, but the divided choir vestry question, supremely unaffected by all her clerical wiles, gradually ceased to sadden her. Her eventual change of heart was all down to the organist, she realized. As the choirladies continually told her, he was the most charming man. Conversation with him was always absolutely delightful, encouraging – flattering. He's even warmly invited her to accompany the choirmen on their next brewery visit and she found herself accepting eagerly . . .

And so the new lady curate finds increasing favour in the parish. And the choir remain happily, safely, free from the threat of togetherness. Semi-united they stand.

15

Tradition

My friend Henry's village church is so historic that, despite being buried in the back of beyond, it yearly draws hundreds of visitors off the beaten track and the church council do a roaring trade selling T-shirts, tea-cloths and keyrings bearing a romantic likeness of the church.

The body of the church has an appropriately historic heating system that only the vicar's warden understands and which, nevertheless, the congregation all agree is very efficient and never gives any trouble (no one and nothing under the vicar's warden's eye ever dares give any trouble). But up in the choir they've never really had a heating system at all and in the winter the choir have depended entirely on the odd oil stove here and there and thick pullovers under their choir robes. No one in the choir ever seems to have complained about this and it has been accepted as part of the very historic set-up. However, recently during the summer months, the vicar's warden was instrumental in having a brand new heating system installed in the choir. A very thorough and determined man, he early on decided that the system should be thoroughly tested in readiness for its winter duties.

Life can be mischievous. The Sunday chosen for the test (a day that coincided with one of my occasional 'guest appearances' in the choir) dawned quite unexpectedly and exceptionally hot for early September – or for any other month for that matter – but the vicar's warden, being so thorough and determined (he is basically a nice man and no one ever calls him stubborn), went ahead, operating the new system at full blast. As the choir processed into the chancel from the cob-webbed coolness of their vestry, a wave of tropical heat met us and enveloped us in the choir stalls. No one seemed to take any notice, however, and we started off matins in our usual rousing manner with one of the vicar's favourite militaristic Victorian hymns all about avenging armies and golden cities.

But from then on the fates were against us. The psalm appointed for that particular Sunday was one of the longest and most repetitive in the book and set to one of the only chants we didn't know by heart, the rest of the hymns appeared to have dozens of seemingly endless verses set to dawdling, unco-operative tunes and the anthem (unaccompanied) seemed to get longer and longer as we ploughed through it, and more and more tuneless and flatter and flatter until it petered out in a sort of discordant groan.

Following this, the vicar extended the prayers by leaving long gaps for what he called individual meditation and private thought, during which the congregation stared about the church and wished he'd get on with it. Then, in an extra-long sermon he went on and on about the laity being the church, not just the clergy. What he seemed to be saying was that he wanted members of the congregation to take over the parish visiting and only bring him into proceedings if some awkward parishioner absolutely insisted on seeing him or threatened to withdraw from the free-will offering scheme.

During the final hymn someone's infant at the back of the church had clearly had enough and started bawling and kicking the pew with astonishing vigour and this encouraged another infant to start kicking another pew with equally astonishing vigour. Those in charge simply smiled proudly at their offspring and went on singing, but the uproar upset the organist to such an extent that he played the organ so loudly he not only drowned the infant protest but also drowned the choir who nevertheless carried on in their usual manner, splendidly ignoring the infants, the organ and hot-house heat.

Immediately after the service I went to the back of the church to speak to a friend in the congregation. Returning to the vestry a few minutes later, I found a few members of the choir still standing around, apparently quite unaffected by the tropically heated matins we had just sung through. Henry brought me into the conversation. 'He's gone off in a huff – said we sang the anthem utterly insensitively – utterly.' I knew who he was talking about. Everyone in the choir always refers to the organist as 'he' or 'him' and has quite happily put up with him for years – like they've put up with the lack of heating – as part of the church's unique historical background.

Actually, I thought we'd sung to our usual standard

for the matins anthem but I realized that this particular anthem had been a special request of the vicar's – a brand new work by someone his wife's cousin knew who was apparently a rising young genius destined to go far – and the organist was very impressed by rising young geniuses destined to go far . . .

There was a short silence while we all thought on this strange huffiness of the organist, then a choirgirl who has a delightful soprano voice – and in the eyes of all the male members of the choir is altogether delightful – flung her choir gown over a tarnished brass rail where a confusion of like gowns had already been flung. 'I don't know what he's making such a fuss about,' she said. 'The congregation never listen to the anthem anyway. The front pews were all asleep before we'd finished this morning.'

'The vicar said it was a very moving piece of music,' remarked a comfortably round tenor, looking up from the headline horror of his Sunday tabloid.

'Moving!' repeated the choirgirl. 'It'd take a jolly sight more than that dirge to move our matins lot. You couldn't move them with a bulldozer. Why, they even go to sleep when vicar does one of his "we must all arise and march forward together" sermons and keeps bashing on the pulpit and bawling.'

'Well, they're used to it,' said Henry. 'They know he's not really upset.' We moved into the churchyard where some of the congregation lingered to gossip in the shade of the trees rather than gossiping in the terribly hot coffee room with the terrible coffee.

A large, obviously important lady who had slept in

the middle of the front pew drifted stately across to the choirgirl. 'That *lovely* anthem,' she purred. 'You all sung it so thrillingly. I was on the edge of my seat *right* through.'

Nothing discomposed the choirgirl. Captivating hazel eyes sparkled. 'Thank you very much,' she beamed.

That evening there took place the traditional Choir Benefit Evensong when the whole congregation are supposed to turn up especially to listen to the choir and, in recognition of their devoted service, put a lot of money into the special collection for the choir's annual outing. The Choir Benefit Evensong has taken place on the second Sunday in September from as far back as anyone in the parish can remember. It is the occasion when, according to the vicar's warden, the choir mercilessly slaughter some of the most beautiful church music ever composed and the vicar gets out of preaching the sermon with the excuse that nothing he can say can possibly compensate for taking up time in which the choir could be 'giving such joy with their glorious singing'.

The congregation are nothing if not loyal to tradition and dutifully fill the church at each Choir Benefit Evensong and thankfully fill the collection bags when at last it's over and they can escape. Only a few actually find it impossible to face the ordeal but the choir outing fund doesn't suffer because the backsliders always pay generous conscience money.

As usual, the Choir Benefit Evensong was a resounding success, with every pew crammed and a very generous sum in the collection. Not that the choir are ever fooled by the apparent demonstration of appreciation by the congregation. As the organist impressed on me after the service, some of his best friends were members of the congregation and they were all utter philistines quite incapable of recognizing beautiful singing. 'The only reason why they stick it listening to the choir for over an hour is because of the free "do" at the vicarage afterwards,' he assured me.

Tradition further dictated that, following the Choir Benefit Evensong, the vicar should entertain both choir and congregation at a jolly celebration at the vicarage. The vicar, always grasping another opportunity for a demonstration of parish 'togetherness', had set to work with a will organizing a team to produce the trestle tables loaded with tiny sausages on sticks, even tinier sandwiches and 'special offer' supermarket wine so dear to the hearts of church party organizers.

Choir and congregation mingled heart-warmingly in the overflowing vicarage drawing room and remarks like '*wonderful* evening', 'really *lovely* singing', 'I listened absolutely *riveted*', and 'I sometimes wonder what it would be like if we didn't have a choir at all', drifted warmly among the genteel crush.

The delightful choirgirl stood near me at the end of a trestle table observing the scene and discreetly consuming three microscopic sandwiches at a time. 'What a wonderful thing tradition is,' she remarked to me, smiling dazzlingly across the room at the vicar's warden who was trying determinedly to photograph her from the midst of the swaying surge of well-wishers around the 'special offer' wine table.

16

The Screen

The Suffolk village church where I am sometimes a guest in the choir is a medieval gem. It is also extremely decrepit and over the last 200 years has been regularly saved from complete collapse by the same highly respected firm of local builders who are ever ready to bodge it up as each desperate emergency arises. Towards the end of the nineteenth century they put up a flamboyant chancel screen, given by a lady who sat in the middle of the front row and was fed up with always having to look at the choirboys' dirty knees which were clearly visible through the open-work choir stalls and button-less cassocks. The church council of the day were very pleased to accept the screen because not only did it hide the dirty knees, it also made it less likely that the venerable and ailing chancel arch would one day fall down all over the choir.

But the present-day new vicar, a worshipper of all things medieval, knew nothing of the history of the practical value of the screen and saw only what he described to a few like-minded cronies as a vulgar Victorian monstrosity. Indeed, after a few months in the parish his horror of the brutal desecration of the medieval gem had grown to an all-out obsession that drove all other parish matters from his mind.

The very word 'Victorian' had always made him shudder. In other parishes where he had served he had constantly to brace himself in the face of philistine choirs and congregations who were ever wanting to sing dreadful gushing Victorian hymns with tunes that seemed to have come straight from the music hall or a smoking concert. He had had to deal with awful parishioners who insisted on retaining and preserving Victorian churchyards crammed with gravestones full of verses about people being gone but not forgotten and singing in celestial choirs. He had even been inveigled into heading a parochial church council committee organizing a scheme for the restoration of a monstrous red and green Victorian stained-glass window depicting St George getting the better of the dragon.

And now, the church screen was the last straw. The new vicar decided to fight. He started to put out feelers. How would people like the very splendid view of the medieval chancel to be fully revealed again, unimpeded by the gross bulk of the Victorian screen? The response from the congregation was meagre. Either they had never realized the medieval splendours of the chancel or they thought that the chancel screen was quite nice. Certainly, few thought it should be removed and most didn't appear to think at all. Only the choir had a firm and unanimous opinion. They were outraged at the idea.

On the bottom panels of the screen were numerous

brass memorial tablets to choristers who had sung in the choir for years and years. What would happen to them if the screen were to be removed? And what would happen to the marrows and cabbages and bags of tomatoes and bundles of onions that were always hung all over the screen at harvest festival? Besides, how could members of the choir carry on reading their Sunday papers and doing things they traditionally did during the sermon if the screen was pulled down to reveal their every movement to the congregation? The whole crazy idea was out of the question.

All this I learned from a letter from the organist, an old school friend who invited me to the village for the weekend of the local horse show, Shire horses being great favourites of mine, together with trams, paddle steamers and the earlier editions of *Hymns Ancient and Modern*. So now, eager to admire the horses and enjoy a good uninhibited sing in the village choir, I arrived in the village.

Discussing the Victorian chancel screen question with my friend the organist over supper it was evident that he was regarding the whole thing very philosophically. After all, as he pointed out, there were always people these days who were anxious to change things and upset the apple cart. A year ago, for instance, there had been trouble with the 'rip-out-the-Victorian-pews' brigade who wanted to replace the pews with those little wooden chairs, presumably made for midgets. There is nowhere to put your hymn book and when you kneel down your heels get trapped under a bar of the chair behind. Then there were some very persistent women who wanted to turn the churchyard into a kiddies' playground with a goldfish pond and sections of concrete sewer pipe to crawl through and a skateboard track all round the church.

There was also a pressure group who felt that the church should be more prominent in the neighbourhood and wanted to frame the noticeboards and the tower clock with red and blue neon tubes, but no one took any notice of them because they mainly belonged to the crowd who persisted in coming to Sunday evensong instead of the family communion service and were regarded by the vicar very much as third-class citizens.

'But, not to worry,' my friend leaned back in his comfortable, although I always think disreputable, old armchair and stretched his legs towards the fire. His tone was unperturbed, reassuring. 'The vicar's just doing his "new broom" act – all new vicars do. He'll never get the screen taken out. We'd have to get a faculty and there would be meetings, arguments, alternative suggestions, letters to the local paper and people resigning from the choir, and the flower committee. Probably, some important character, organizing a rally in the churchyard before matins or a sit-down strike in front of the screen at evensong, would drop dead and we'd all be back where we started – no, the vicar'll never get that screen thrown out.'

The next day my friend and I arrived early at church for Sunday matins to find the vicar apparently driving a small, middle-aged, rather startled looking man up and down the aisle in a most relentless manner. The vicar was in full flood and appeared to be reaching a climax of fiery exaltation to the little man to behold and marvel at the glories of his medieval surroundings. As we approached he towered over his victim and demanded, 'Have you ever seen anything so inspiring in a mere village church – badly treated by time but still so superb, so pure?' He raised his hands dramatically towards the roof and held a brief silence. The little man grabbed his chance.

'My grandfather sang in the choir here for 60 years,' he piped. 'I believe there is a memorial to him somewhere in the church. Can you show me? Name of Hodge. I want to take a photograph. I'm on holiday from New Zealand.'

The vicar slowly lowered his arms. He looked bewildered, as if he didn't know where he was.

My friend stepped forward. 'Let me show you,' he invited the little man. We all gathered at one end of the chancel screen at the foot of which was the memorial to one Hodge, a mighty Victorian bass, a pillar of the choir cricket team – a great man.

The vicar recovered enough to join us round the plaque. 'A splendid record,' he murmured, and smiled bravely.

'And a splendid place for a memorial to be,' responded the little man. 'What a lovely screen.' It transpired that he sang alto in his church choir in New Zealand, so he joined us in the choir for matins. He said afterwards he'd never enjoyed a service so much. My friend the organist said he was very pleased to hear it. At the family service on Sundays the vicar always had his way with the singing of hymns that were new and meaningful and related to today's vital problems and aspirations. The psalm too was always a modern re-hash that was also meaningful and related. But at matins the congregation and choir had their way, and the vicar, feeling very democratic and forgiving, endured the kind of music that the bass, Hodge, would have thundered out in the 1890s and that the present singers still championed.

New Zealand had been kind to the little man and prospered him, and the little man was now kind to his grandfather's church. Before he returned to New Zealand a few days later he handed the vicar a cheque of considerable value. He asked that the money should go towards the restoration of the church – including attention to the screen, which seemed to be scarred and knocked about in places.

Eighteen months later he was with us again at a special thanksgiving service for the restoration made possible by his generosity. Much good work had been done on the tower and the magnificent nave roof and the chancel arch – and the screen, repolished, regilded, restored to its cheerful Victorian splendour, guarded the choir with a new authority.

The vicar was overjoyed at the results of the unexpected help. He tries to perpetuate his enjoyment by not looking at the newly glittering chancel screen, but people keep saying how lovely it is and this makes him sad at times. But he soon cheers up. Recently a publisher invited him to contribute a key article to a forthcoming, very learned book on medieval church architecture and he is now so busy and delighted and elated that brash Victorian screens and awful Victorian choirs are almost beneath his notice.

17

The Superb Choir

When a choir, choirmaster and organist work together as a team, all generally goes well with them and the only threat of disharmony comes from the vicar. Vicars normally fall into two categories – those who insist on being the power behind the throne and dictate the musical policy of the church down to the final amen, and those who are only too pleased to let the choir get on with it as long as they don't do anything too outrageous and upset the more prickly members of the congregation. These latter vicars are well liked by choirs and can depend on solid backing from members for just anything they want to do in the parish as long as it has nothing to do with the music. The former types are resented by the choir and are apt to receive vitriolic notes and phone calls from members, to which they reply in equally unpleasant and unbending tones, until either the organist and choirmaster or the vicar resigns, or the whole choir walk out and invade a neighbouring church choir – who don't want them.

Such a calamity recently overtook the very happy choir of which my friend Wally is organist and choirmaster. The vicar at Wally's church has been there for years and years and is definitely of the 'leave 'em alone' brigade as far as the choir is concerned. His only connection with the music is his part in singing the versicles, which he's never been able to accomplish without going flat. He doesn't *know* he goes flat – he's such a pleasant man that nobody ever tells him. Consequently life has flowed smoothly for Wally's choir and they enjoy the affection of the congregation for the comfortably familiar. It must be said, of course, and Wally himself would agree, that his is not a choir of exalted standards. They mainly lead the congregation in the singing of favourite hymns and perform a jolly rumbustious Victorian anthem or two at Christmas, Easter and harvest. They've never entered a choral competition or performed at a concert, and the only singing they ever do outside the church is when they go round the pubs at Christmas singing carols in aid of a local old people's home and a sanctuary for retired horses.

On the other hand, the choir of the neighbouring parish church are superb. Indeed they are always referred to in the local paper and by members themselves as superb. The opening services of local arts festivals and prestigious civic occasions are by general consent held at this church so that the event may be graced by the performance of the superb choir, and no one with any artistic pretensions at all would go anywhere else to get married.

The superb choir are always busy giving impeccable recitals and winning choral competitions all over the place. In fact, they are often so busy that they are not able to find time to sing at the actual church services, but the congregation have always realized that the inconvenience is a small price to pay for such a superb choir.

It was the advent of a new vicar at the parish church that upset everything recently. He seemed to think that, superb or not, church choirs were meant mainly to sing at church services and shouldn't be too annoyed if the congregation's singing was not up to standard and flawed the superb sound of the choir. The new vicar decreed that forthwith the choir should sing at every choral service, despite the pressing calls of recitals, competitions and festivals.

He outraged the whole choir. They simply could not conceive how anyone could be such a philistine as to try to impede such a superb choir from spreading abroad their superb act. The choirmaster promptly withdrew his choir from the church. Looking around with a professional eye, he lighted on Wally's church as the one with best acoustics for miles. There and then he decided that this church should instantly benefit from the singing of his superb choir.

Thus it was that one Sunday evening immediately after evensong the vestry of Wally's church was invaded by the whole superb choir. Their choirmaster had a word with the vicar, who promptly passed him on to Wally and hurried away down the church to shake hands with the congregation. Even before he had properly cornered Wally behind the vestry piano, the choirmaster was imparting the good news of the advent of his choir. It would, he explained, enable Wally and his singers to achieve things undreamed of far, far beyond mere hymn-singing. A whole new world would be opened up. They would be thrilled. He had got deep into details of when and how future choir rehearsals would take place under the new regime before Wally succeeded in halting him in mid-sentence to say no, thank you very much. But if any members of the superb choir would like to join his choir and learn how to sing hymns properly, they would be welcome – and indeed especially welcome to come and swell the crowd at the carol-singing round the pubs at Christmas.

Stunned, the choirmaster regarded Wally, aghast. What was the Church of England coming to? Everywhere there were philistines – philistines wherever you looked. Was there no appreciation of the higher things any more – no respect – no ambition? He moved away amid his shocked singers.

'Choir practice seven-thirty Fridays,' called Wally after them. 'We always have a good sing.'

Having seen off the last of the congregation, the vicar returned hesitantly to the vestry and seemed surprised that no members of the superb choir were in evidence. 'All – er – fixed up then?' He switched a general smile in Wally's direction. 'I – er – gather that they plan to join our choir. Some little bother at the parish church, I believe.'

Wally put him right on the situation, concluding, 'So we won't be seeing *them* again.' The vicar visibly brightened up as the company left the church for their evening television viewing or rather more colourful argument at the Dog and Duck. The vicar, however, had not heard the last of the affair. The next evening a worried vicar of the parish church telephoned him with an urgent appeal. No doubt he had heard of the annoying business of his choir's walking out. In a way he was rather glad they'd gone – he wouldn't have to sit through any more 20-minute anthems or be expected to enjoy singing favourite hymns to tunes he'd never heard of – but the immediate difficulty was that there was an important choral wedding booked for Saturday and he simply couldn't present the party with no organ or empty choir stalls. Could his colleague's choir and organist help out?

As was his wont in circumstances like these, Wally's vicar passed the parish church vicar straight on to Wally. 'You'll catch him in if you phone him immediately,' he urged, and put the phone down quickly. He'd done his bit. Whatever the outcome, he would smile and say he was sure it was for the best. He settled down happily to his book on steam traction in the nineteenth century.

Meanwhile, the vicar of the parish church, who had never heard Wally's choir sing and knew nothing whatsoever about them, was telling Wally over the phone how privileged he would feel to have such a choir singing at the wedding on Saturday, and Wally, who was thinking that after all it would make a change from singing round the pubs, was waiting for a break in the flow of flattery to say yes. He enjoyed wedding services. He was always intrigued by the unbelievable hats chosen by the mothers of the bride and groom, and by the behaviour of guests who were not used to being in church, who either tiptoed everywhere and tended to bow to everyone in a cassock, or bawled across the church to each other as if they were at a football match.

Wally's choir backed him magnificently on Saturday. Every member was present at the parish church, where the vicar treated them with a deference and overwhelming friendliness that even surprised him. Indeed, he hadn't finished his speech of welcome before he suddenly realized that it was almost time for the wedding party to arrive and, apologizing profusely, trotted off to do some more welcoming in the church porch.

Some members of the choir were leafing through the music to be sung. A large bass with a scrubbed, shiny red face and cigarette butt wedged behind his ear rumbled, 'What's this Latin thing? We don't do this kind of stuff at weddings. We don't do it at all – not Latin stuff.'

Wally reassured him and the rest of the choir. 'Don't worry about that. It's all in unison, anyway. I'll play it on the organ and you follow where you can. You'll soon pick it up.'

'And then, this hymn,' persisted the bass. 'We know the words but I bet no one's heard the tune.'

Wally gave it a brief glance as he adjusted his large spotted bow tie before the equally spotted vestry mirror. 'That's all right,' he said, and raising his voice above the usual winter-sale din that always rose from his choir as the time of a service approached, 'we'll do our tune to the first hymn. And the final amen looks a funny kind of thing. Forget it. We'll do Stainer's sevenfold. Can't beat the old sevenfold. And I'll play 'em out with the French thing you like,' he concluded comfortably.

'The thing that sounds like the Wurlitzer down at

the Odeon when I was a lad,' clarified the big bass. 'Just the job. They'll like that.'

Whether anybody in the wedding party ever realized that the original choice of music had been revamped is doubtful. The wedding was one of those high fashion affairs, the sun shone brightly, and afterwards, during the photography session in the churchyard, everyone kept falling over half-submerged gravestones and exclaiming 'Lovely!' and 'Gorgeous!' and 'Jolly good show!'

Wally was sure that they were talking about the choir, a belief heightened by the vicar who, providing against the possibility of the superb choir never returning to the fold, assured Wally that he'd *never* enjoyed singing with a choir so much – particularly the first hymn to that grand old tune he hadn't heard since the days he'd been a choirboy. Later he was surprised to realize that he'd really meant every word he'd said.

And having failed to gatecrash any other churches, the superb choir did return to the parish church and, despite all their other engagements, they do now manage to sing at all the Sunday services. Just occasionally, however, a very important concert engagement does clash with a wedding and then the parish church vicar happily, indeed eagerly, phones Wally and Wally and his choir roll up and put on another jolly good show of the vicar's kind of music.

18

Mud with Pug

The rector was definitely a man's man, a robust outdoor type. His teenage daughter strikingly resembled him. She was called Pug and wore her hair in the style of an ill-used mop, shapeless clothes and what are known as 'sensible' shoes.

I had located the rectory some half a mile from the village church and had called to ask if I might sing in the choir that evening. The rector had readily consented, but had appeared a little disconcerted, I thought, when he learned that I was an alto. 'The *girls* sing that line in our choir,' he said. 'The *men* sing tenor or bass.' However, he invited me to stay for tea and accompany his daughter and himself to church afterwards.

Throughout the meal he told me all about the crafty church council who were always holding up his plans for changing the services, the times of the services, and the hymn book. He also spoke with awe about the veteran organist who wouldn't even listen to his plans. He made it clear, however, that everyone concerned was a 'good sort' and that he admired people who stick to their guns. Indeed, he became so enthusiastic about people sticking to their guns that Pug had to warn him that unless he gave over soon we should be late for evensong.

The rector thereupon took off his slippers and put on the largest pair of boots I'd ever seen. He explained that although a bus was due in a few minutes, we should walk to the church because generally speaking the bus failed to materialize, and in any case it was more invigorating and interesting to take the short cut across the fields to church.

Pug had another reason. The original church, she said, was a very fine fourteenth-century building, but during the last century some ham-handed vandal had 'restored' the interior so thoroughly that it was completely ruined. Ever ready to defend the Victorians I mildly suggested that had the ham-handed vandal not restored it, it would probably have fallen down by now anyway. She scorned this unfashionable thought. She considered that the only *bearable* way to view the church nowadays was at a distance from the field behind the graveyard. 'There is a full moon tonight,' she enthused. 'We shall get a *superb* view.'

She now donned a disreputable duffle coat while the rector disappeared into an even more appalling relic. Leaving by the back door the rector led us up the garden path. I don't know what had happened to the full moon, for apart from being shudderingly cold and windy the night was pitch black. Large pieces of unsuspected meat fat gently stroked my face as we passed under a tree by the gate. Pug said she hung them there for the birds, and she hoped I hadn't knocked any down. Lumbering ahead into a ploughed field the rector continued his monologue about the church council and the organist, but I didn't gather very much of what he bellowed because I couldn't keep up with him for long and the wind was howling in the wrong direction.

At the far side of the field we came upon a five-barred gate over which the rector and Pug quickly vaulted, and I quickly fell and tore my raincoat. Pug forged ahead, and I made a desperate effort to keep astride of the rector. This was almost impossible as my low shoes had now filled with earth and stones, and were no match for his magnificent clodhoppers, but I felt that as a guest I should at least try to show a little interest in my host's views. 'We have a great musical tradition,' he was roaring, 'tradition of good robust congregational singing. Organist pulls out all the stops and everybody else throws in all they've got and tries to drown him. Sort of friendly competition. Works wonders with the hymns and gets over the awkward bits in the psalms.'

He ceased for a moment to grab unsuccessfully at my arm as I tripped over a tree root and fell down an unsuspected bank. As I picked myself up Pug re-appeared and told me we had now reached the local river. This was an evil-looking mess bounded on either side by dead trees, crouched against the skyline like monsters from an Edgar Allan Poe nightmare. Pug said this was a most beautiful spot to spend a long summer evening . . .

The rector joined me again, and started to explain his plans for getting round the organist's unreasonable objections to changing the hymn book and cutting out hymns referring to celestial choirs singing for ever and ever. But by this time I was so dispirited that I couldn't even trouble to stick to my guns and declare myself all for the organist.

'Here we are,' bawled Pug, from nearby, and I saw that she was untying a half waterlogged wreck of a rowing boat. She splashed into it, followed by the rector who seized two broken oars. 'Don't sit on the back seat,' she advised me jovially, 'it's full of the jolly old woodworm.' There was no other seat available so I lowered myself cosily to the bottom of the boat in what she would doubtlessly have called the jolly old moisture.

We floundered to a halt in the mud on the opposite bank and started to climb one of those banks that amateurs can only negotiate on their hands and knees. As I crawled by his side the rector said that he had at last persuaded the organist to use a new tune for 'Fight the Good Fight' and I should have the pleasure of hearing it tonight. 'It's a step in the right direction,' he gloated, as I slipped backwards down the bank.

Some minutes later as we crossed the last field of our short cut, Pug's voice sung out ahead of us. 'Well, what do you think of *that*!' She was, I suppose, pointing to the church, but I couldn't see a thing. I didn't even see the half-filled swill bucket that someone had thoughtfully left in the middle of the path . . .

And then, unbelievably, I stood in the vestry, a muddy disgrace to all altos. Pug's sensible shoes and the rector's brutish boots showed not the slightest fleck of dirt. There is something in knowing every inch of your countryside. The organist regarded me as he must have often regarded the worst juvenile delinquents in his choir. 'There's some water and a broom in the porch. They might help,' he said doubtfully.

As I crept from his presence trying to persuade myself that I should soon wake up, I heard him apologizing to the rector. 'So sorry about the new tune for tonight. I've left the copies at home. Can't think how I came to do it.'

Somehow, deep down, I felt cheered.

19

Something for Everyone

My friend Sid's village church choir is not what you'd call professional; it's just very enthusiastic and cheerful – and, according to the vicar, whose personal musical world is all plainchant and unaccompanied medieval murmurings, somewhat boisterous. Indeed, in his more desperate moments, in the company only of two or three trusted churchwardens, after having endured one of the choir's thunderous festival choral evensongs, the vicar has been known to describe it as a prime example of brute force and ignorance.

Unusually, the other evening at choir practice, which Sid has conducted for the past 40 years, he was explaining to the girl sopranos what he meant by singing softly. 'When I says S-O-F-T,' he clarified, 'I don't mean stop altogether. I mean just calm down a bit so that we can get a contrast with the really beefy bit on the last page of the anthem. You can really let it go then.'

A little nut-brown man hardly taller than the vestry piano, Sid peered affectionately over his half glasses at his dozen loyal supporters whose ages ranged from eight to 80. He turned to an outsized youth who until a few months ago had shrieked treble in the front row and whose voice, having lately broken, was now hooting a wild kind of alto in the back row. 'You're a big lad now,' said Sid, 'and you've got a very big voice. That's fine, but just keep it down a bit. We don't want it a yard wide when you're standing right next to the vicar on Sunday. He's never been very musical ... he doesn't appreciate ... and we don't want any trouble.'

Sid likes good sturdy singing and he plays the organ in a good sturdy way too. In fact, he plays it so sturdily that even a chorister without confidence and who doesn't know the music is encouraged to sing in a gloriously uninhibited manner. Within living memory the congregation have always enjoyed their music dispensed in this manner – indeed, one could say revelled in it – and although, over the years, a succession of vicars has weighed in with their own ideas, all of which differed widely from those of Sid's choir, no one has ever made the slightest impression and all have soon come to realize the truth of the saying 'If you can't beat 'em, join 'em' – even to the extreme extent of accompanying the choir in their annual summer outing to some coastal resort selected for its preponderance of pubs and funfairs.

It was after the latest of these outings that the emergency arose. It was noted that during the outward journey the vicar sat at the back of the coach, looking even more bewildered and dejected than he usually appeared on such occasions, and closed his eyes and sighed even more often. At the resort he only picked at his fish and chips and, on the homeward journey, refused potato crisps, chocolates and canned beer, and joined in the tumultuous choruses hardly at all. When the party arrived back in the village he assured everyone how much – indeed, how *very* much – he had enjoyed the splendid day and disappeared up the vicarage drive before anyone else could struggle out of the coach. The next morning, Sunday, he had reported sick.

And now the hour of Sunday matins was approaching and there was no one to conduct it. Even the local retired priest was not available, having gone fishing with the latest Ruth Rendell and a large steak and kidney pie. Members of the choir and some churchwardens and sidesmen stood around in the churchyard assessing the situation. 'Anyone can conduct matins,' said a cheerful-looking little man, who had recently come to live in the village. 'It's not like communion, when you need a priest. In the parish where I was in London, we used to have all kinds of people taking matins – our local doctor, the captain of the bell-ringers, the mayor – just anybody – women . . . it didn't matter at all.'

As the others heard these words, there was a frozen silence. Then Sid put things right. 'Well, we're not having just anybody taking our matins,' he declared, and there was a visible relaxing of tension. It relaxed even further when one of Sid's tenors, who ran the local garage and possessed some kind of magic that transformed written-off car wrecks into going concerns, said, 'There's this parson who's on holiday and had a bit of an accident with his car – smashed it to bits down a dyke. I fixed it for him and he's collecting it at half-past nine. He might do.'

Half the parish were down at the tenor's garage to

look over the man who might do. He was so excited and delighted at the way his wreck had been transformed ('Looks better than I've ever seen it!') that he was indeed eager to oblige in any way he could. He was a big, middle-aged, humorous-looking man who asked to be called Ted, and he kept on circling his little car and patting it, sighing gustily and repeating, 'Matins at eleven o'clock? Yes, certainly, wonderful, wonderful.' Although whether he meant matins was wonderful or the job on his car was not quite certain.

The little car was given a place of honour outside the lych-gate, a place normally reserved for Sid's motorbike, and the beaming volunteer was escorted into the church and given details of the service procedure. His delight grew. 'This is a marvellous place,' he exclaimed, still unable to remove completely his gaze from his restored four-wheeled friend, clearly seen through the west doorway. 'Everything out of the Prayer Book, it seems, and good old Ancient and Modern. No special do-it-yourself service on a leaflet. No extra "songs" on bits of paper – and my old travelling companion brought back from the dead. What more can a man ask? What a delightful place.'

He possessed a huge basso profundo voice and was a worthy addition to Sid's choir, and when he went into the pulpit he had no need of the church's faltering relay system. He said how lucky we were to belong to the Church of England where, these days, members can find almost any kind of service they can imagine, from meditation to dancing in the aisles. He said the goings-on in the last church he had visited, for instance, were rather different from those he was now enjoying. He had had a most enlightening experience in southern England.

Apparently the vicar of that church had explained, for the sake of first-time attendees, that he firmly believed that hymns could not be sung meaningfully unless the words were accompanied by joyous action. Ted was supplied with a booklet of special hymns that the vicar said were relevant praise for today and consisted of a line or so of basic words repeated three or four times for each verse. And while you yelled these out – the vicar kept on bawling 'Come on, raise the roof!' – you had to perform the joyous action by clapping and stamping and whirling round and round and smiling at everyone. Ted said that all those around him seemed to be thoroughly enjoying themselves, but the whole thing got him so giddy that by the time they'd reached the sixth verse of the first hymn he was not even sure where he was, let alone who he was smiling at. But everyone was very jolly and after the service kept handing him cups of coffee and large sticky biscuits made by someone called Pearl, and numerous leaflets about future happy get-togethers in the church.

After they'd seen off their providential visitor, still purring over the miracle of his renewed little car, Sid and some of his choir repaired to The Raven, their usual Sunday rendezvous after matins, where discussions turned on Ted's sermon. 'Imagine swivelling round and round and clapping hands in our choir stalls,' said Sid. 'How could you keep your eye on the music?'

'Most of the time we don't look at the music,' confessed the car-restoring tenor, 'but swivelling round and round – I wonder why they do that?'

An attractive choirgirl broke off from telling the landlord's outsized Boxer dog what a 'booful boy' he was and said, 'Rapturous joy. It's supposed to be because of rapturous joy.'

'It'd be a very noisy kind of rapturous joy in our choir stalls,' said Sid, 'what with the hollow wooden floors and no carpets on 'em.'

'And smiling right through the hymn – it must be hard to smile right through a hymn if you're not used to it,' suggested the tenor. 'It would need a lot of practice.'

'People smile at me all the time,' said the attractive choirgirl, 'lots of them.' She patted the huge solidity of 'booful boy'. 'Look, even he's smiling.'

'I don't see what it's got to do with hymn-singing,' pursued the tenor. 'When I was a choirboy you got it in the neck if you smiled at people when you were supposed to be singing.'

'Times have changed, I reckon,' mused Sid. 'Thank goodness they haven't changed here, though. What if our choir had to turn itself into a religious pop group and dance in the aisles?'

'We wouldn't be as bad as that terrible lot that play down at the community centre,' said the attractive choirgirl, 'but they don't smile – they just pull awful faces.'

'I remember my niece telling me about a church where they had to stamp their feet when they sang hymns,' recounted the tenor. 'She said the trouble was that the kids caught on to the idea in a big way and went on stamping like mad right through the service.'

'Anyway, what about the hymns for next Sunday?' asked Sid. 'We haven't had "Rock of Ages" for a long time.'

20

We Shall Not Be Moved

They don't like change at the village church in a secret part of Wiltshire where my cousin George sings in the choir. (It's a secret because the railway company have never heard of it and no bus can seem to find its way there even once a week.) Everybody and everything at the church has been the same for at least 40 years – except the present vicar. He has been there for only ten years and so is always referred to as the New Vicar; his predecessor who held the post for the regulation 40 years is still naturally talked of as the Vicar.

'We have a bit of trouble with the New Vicar now and again,' George explained to me one evening during a short holiday I was spending with him in the village. 'He has these funny ideas about altering things, but the church council soon put him right. And of course, like so many of these new men, he often has a go at the choir – says we sing too much Victorian music and why don't we sometimes sing some of the nice modern hymns, so much more relevant to today's vital thinking in the church, which he has gummed into the front of our Ancient and Moderns.' George says that the organist, a splendidly flamboyant octogenarian who still wears spats on Sundays and has a large picture of Wagner pinned up over the organ console, refuses to have anything to do with these hymns because he reckons that you can't tell whether they're relevant to today's vital thinking or not, as they all seem to consist of one line repeated three times followed by a chorus of one word repeated four times.

The New Vicar thinks that the organist and the choir are biased. Certainly, he suffers a lot from the activities of the choir. No matter how kindly and diplomatically he admonishes them (and he is a very kindly and diplomatic young man) the choir still keeps on singing long, uproarious Victorian anthems that absolutely shatter his nerves and addle his thoughts on higher things. In desperation he once suggested that the choir should sing an entire service of modern meaningful music just once a quarter, but the church council turned the idea down flat – so the New Vicar carries on suffering.

Each time I visit George and arrive in the vestry as a guest in the choir the New Vicar dutifully bears down on me and shakes my hand and says things like, 'Well, well, so here we are again. So nice to have you with us to help swell the joyful sound.' But on this particular Sunday morning he was looking positively thrilled and beamed at everybody, even the organist. George explained that this was because just before my arrival he had heard that the only alto in the choir had suddenly succumbed to flu and consequently it would not be possible to perform the anthem. Alas, how short-lived can real happiness be! When he realized that I, in fact, sung a sort of alto – till then apparently, what I did in the choir had been a mystery to him – and that the anthem could therefore now go ahead, he stoically held his cheerful smile and said, 'Good, splendid! Yes, indeed.'

Matins proceeded at a rollicking pace. After an exhilarating streak through the psalms and canticles we roared through a splendid Victorian anthem full of lush duets and rousing bass solos and a final pounding chorus. When we ended in a truly deafening burst of sound – probably rather more deafening than the composer had intended – the New Vicar, who has to brace himself to face up to the choir's singing of even a quiet Victorian anthem, and is given to humming some of his favourite 'simple, beautiful new hymns' during other people's sermons, took quite a few moments to recover sufficiently to breathe, 'Let us pray.' But so upset was he that he started intoning well-remembered prayers from the Book of Common Prayer instead of the modern prayers he had managed against great odds to slip into the services, which constituted his single victory over the church council in ten years. The realization of the awful reactionary thing he had done flustered him still further and he announced the wrong hymn. Nobody took any notice of him and we all sang the right hymn, which was all about golden cities and celestial choirs and people in white robes with harps. The organist plainly enjoyed this so much that he completely drowned out the choir and the congregation – who were singing in a magnificent football crowd unison – in the last verse and easily obliterated the squeaking of the New Vicar's white and grey gym shoes on the polished black and orange Victorian tiles as he made his way to the pulpit.

I am not quite sure what the sermon was about. I think it was something to do with the vicar's plans for taking out all the church pews to make the space more flexible for special events such as a motorcyclists' service (including the motorcycles) that he was thinking of arranging to attract the younger element in the parish. But my attention was somewhat distracted by two choirmen next to me who were having an enthusiastic conversation about a steam traction engine rally they were going to on Easter Monday. And as I am infinitely more fascinated by steam traction engines than by motorbikes I'm afraid I didn't follow the sermon beyond the removal of the pews, although George did assure me afterwards that of course the pews would not be removed. The New Vicar, he said, conceived sweeping ideas in rapid succession and his enthusiasm for each new inspiration was so concentrated that he immediately forgot all about the previous one. So there was never much cause for alarm and everyone carried on quite happily.

Anyway, we eventually came to the last hymn, during the singing of which a forbidding military moustached gentleman in a black suit thrust a large brass collection plate around the congregation at a tremendous speed while the organist seemed to be increasing the tempo of the hymn at every line. Indeed, I was becoming quite breathless. I subsequently learned from George that this was all part of a revered tradition in which the choir tried to finish the hymn before the sidesman could get the collection up to the vicar. In turn the sidesman endeavoured to pip the choir to the post by delivering the collection before the choir reached the last verse. In this instance the sidesman won handsomely and obviously the victory meant a great deal to him, from the way his forbidding expression melted into one of real Christian joy as he winked largely at his rivals.

After the service, to the accompaniment of a thunderous organ voluntary that the organist had cobbled together from 'The Twilight of the Gods', the congregation filed out through the elegant west doorway into the immaculate churchyard in a leisurely and dignified manner and the New Vicar shook hands with everyone in a most friendly guise. At the back of the choir vestry the choir shoved out through a battered doorway discreetly hidden behind an exuberant mass of stinging nettles, dead flowers and broken dustbins and nobody shook hands in a friendly or any other way. 'Great service, that,' pronounced George as we picked our way through the dustbins. 'Something you could really get your teeth into.'

A grinding noise came from behind us and the organist hailed us, pushing the vintage bicycle that was one of the well-known sights of the village. It was said that he got it for ten shillings and a set of cigarette cards before World War Two and that on dark nights he still used its original oil lamp. He repeated warm thanks to me for stepping into the breach and on learning that I'd also be coming to evensong he said gleefully that we could repeat the anthem. He'd mention it to the New Vicar . . .

At the church door the New Vicar was still shaking hands with the departing congregation (including one enthusiastic little lady who kept on shaking hands and then going to the back of the queue to shake hands again) and enduring the many compliments paid to the choir about 'the really lovely anthem'. He beamed and desperately looked forward to the quiet of his study where as usual on Sunday afternoon he would recover from the effects of matins by immersing himself in the writings of the new suffragan bishop who was very forward-thinking and appeared as often as possible in jeans and a T-shirt.

From the direction of the choir vestry the familiar rattling sound came nearer. Astride the famous bike the organist waved to the New Vicar, and unbelievingly the New Vicar heard himself calling out, 'Splendid effort with the anthem.' But the organist was not riding away as he normally did. He turned his bike towards the New Vicar.

'Ah, Vicar,' he said, grinding to a halt. 'About evensong tonight . . .'

21

The Invisible Genius

One of my most unbelievable experiences was during a visit to a church deep in the border country of Monmouthshire a few years ago. It was a very old, very big church, lit by gas-lamps that were switched on by electricity. As soon as I noticed this I thought that here was no ordinary set-up. And it wasn't!

Having been invited to join the choir for my one Sunday's stay in the town, I arrived good and early for matins. The entrance to the vestry involved one little step up, followed immediately by another little step down. This was a special device designed to hurtle the unwary visitor head first into the place, thereby affording some harmless amusement for the choirboys.

But there were no choirboys in the vestry just then. Two men sat on a form, under a clock with no hands. One was the local undertaker, and was very jolly. Rising, he shook my hand, said he was a bass, and seemed to be measuring me up with a professional eye. The other man, whom I can only call the Ancient One, didn't attempt to raise himself, or even his eyes, but grated at me, 'Tenor or bass?' When I replied that I was an alto he looked either shocked or disgusted, but I couldn't quite make out which because his face was almost hidden in the *News of the World*.

Just then a large woman of uncertain age lightly negotiated the trick steps. She was a contralto, I learned. (It's funny how so many contraltos are large women of uncertain age.) She was very businesslike, and asked me what I was. Presuming she referred to my voice, I said 'Alto.' Whereupon she, like the Ancient One, appeared either shocked or disgusted and took no more notice of me.

It was now fully 10.35, and as the service was supposed to start at 10.30, the choir began to arrive in earnest. Everybody soon managed to find his or her robes, on somebody else's peg or on the floor, and all 20 of us were ready in a big huddle at the chancel door when the vicar ambled in to start proceedings.

Suddenly a loud gurgling noise filled the vestry, and an attractive soprano, noticing the consternation of my face, explained, 'It's the water – it blows the organ.' She was right, no doubt, but it sounded to me more like blowing a hurricane. Anyway, the organist played so loudly as we processed in that all other sounds were lost, so that was all right.

When he had subsided, and we were safely installed in the chancel, the undertaker, who had started to suck a peppermint, slid a pile of books along the stall to me – a veteran *English Hymnal*, an A & M with no cover, an *Old Cathedral Psalter* which fully lived up to its name, and an early number of *Schoolgirls' Own*. The vicar announced the first hymn, 'Through the night of doubt and sorrow'. And the organist broke forth joyously again at breakneck speed, before anyone had found the place.

A splendidly unconventional character was this man. Apparently he had nothing whatever to do with the choir and worked quite independently. Either they had upset him a long time ago, and he had given them up as a bad job, or he had just grown forgetful. I was told later that only the oldest members even remembered what he looked like, for he hadn't peeped round the curtain in the organ loft for years.

We all finished the hymn round about the same time, and things went quite smoothly until we reached the Benedictus. Then I became completely fogged. The undertaking bass kindly pointed out the chant to me, and the organist kindly played an entirely different one. In the manner of basses the undertaker bawled on regardlessly, but the attractive soprano, who knew about blowing organs with water, turned round and said that the organist *did* sometimes change the chants, and that the one he was now playing wasn't in the book. By this time the choirboys had settled down to their own devices, kneeling devoutly and reading their comics under the book-rests. The rest of us were still quite keen, however, but there seemed to be a little misunderstanding about the responses. The invisible genius in the organ loft apparently decided that contrary to custom they should be sung unaccompanied. This manoeuvre *did* catch everyone on the wrong foot, and so the first three responses were both unaccompanied and unsung.

But we rallied splendidly in the singing of the next hymn. It was something deep and obscure from the

English Hymnal, and went to a tune on a separate manuscript that someone had forgotten to give out. Undaunted, some tenors opposite me rendered the whole thing in a high unison so heartily that we all joined in – even the boys.

The acoustics of the church must have been a trifle defective, because from the choir stalls it was quite impossible to hear what the vicar was saying in the sermon. And it wasn't the fault of any noise in the choir, because all the boys and even some of the women were very quiet, reading their comics, and most of the men had settled down for a nap. I couldn't get interested in my copy of *Schoolgirls' Own*, and found a fascination in surreptitiously watching the congregation who apparently *could* hear the sermon. They were all awake, and I think some were finding the next hymn, which they had no intention of singing. The others looked grateful for a sit-down, and were quite happy.

We finished strongly with 'Glorious things of Thee are spoken', and the organist was so carried away by Haydn's famous tune that he played an extra verse. We all acted quickly, however, and sung the last verse over again – all except the attractive soprano in front of me. She sang the first verse again.

We processed out in a very attractive shambles, the boys and women neck and neck in front, and the bass undertaker bringing up the rear in his most professional manner. The town outside was completely dead at this hour, so most of the adult members made their way to the Conservative Club for a drink, and the boys started a fight in the graveyard.

As I left, the Ancient One, still clutching the *News of the World*, told me aggressively that I'd have to go a long way to meet up with another choir like theirs. I agreed.

22

The Pack-'em-in Church

They called it the Pack-'em-in Church. My friend who invited me to sing in the choir explained that a new forward-looking vicar was livening up proceedings, and congregations had grown to phenomenal sizes. It didn't seem to matter whether anyone knew why they were there or what was going on. The idea was simply to 'pack-'em-in'. The church was suburban Victorian and quite unremarkable, but it was impossible to miss it – or rather it was impossible to miss its noticeboard. This was a huge coloured cinema effort covered with stars and exclamation marks and bearing such thrilling announcements as 'Coming shortly! – Father Bill Bloggs with his electric guitar'.

It was indeed the variety that drew such large congregations. Sunday evensong had gradually developed into a 'popular' service where all kinds of delightful innovations were introduced so that the young people wouldn't become bored. My friend said that on one occasion recently he had gone home voiceless from an impromptu hymn-singing session in which they had bawled through 24 hymns without a stop. On another he had been deafened by a religious jazz get-together that had taken the place of the sermon, and on another had been completely bewildered by a man who for some reason had talked for two hours on wildlife in Outer Mongolia. People turned up in their scores to see what could possibly happen next.

There was an orthodox choir, but the only reason they still functioned was because no one quite knew what to do with them. They were a relic from the bad old days when congregations actually expected to follow a set service. Much to the consternation of the forward-looking vicar, the choir continued to attend each Sunday, but he bore it bravely and tried to make out they weren't there.

On the evening of my visit the organist welcomed me and wished me luck. He explained that as far as he knew we should get as far as the Nunc Dimittis without things going haywire, but one could never tell. He hoped I'd be able to make out what was happening because he himself often got lost and it was a question of using one's initiative. Apparently the vicar never acquainted him with his plans for a service, but the organist admitted quite freely that this did not offend him in the least. In the revered tradition of organists he never took any notice of what the vicar said anyway. The new vicar merely simplified things for him.

Presently he excused himself, and disappeared into the organ loft to render his brief pre-service recital. This had always been much appreciated by the congregation because it tipped them off that the service was about to start and gave them time to stop gossiping and sort themselves out.

The vicar certainly missed much by spurning the choir. They were the most congenial, considerate crowd I had met for a long time. The principal tenor in particular was almost embarrassingly solicitous. He asked me whether I'd rather sit at the end of a choir stall or at the top. If you sat at the end you caught a draught through the memorial window fit to cut your head off, but on the other hand, at the top you were right next to the prehistoric organ-blowing motor that made such a noise you couldn't hear yourself sing. I have a curious aversion to draughts and so elected to cope with the motor.

We marched into church, followed by the vicar who beamed at his tightly packed flock, and a jolly young curate who also beamed. He had been specially imported to attract the teenagers, and specialized in playing a jazzed-up version of 'Abide with me' on a saxophone.

The vicar gained a point over the choir with the very first hymn. Announcing it he enthused, 'Let us sing *energetically* to that joyous new tune we learned at our congregational practice last week. Now! All together!' No one in the choir felt in the least energetic about that particular joyous tune. They had not been invited to the congregational practice, and they'd never even heard of the tune. In any case, it wasn't in their books. Consequently there was a blessed silence from the chancel, except from one very deaf and ancient bass who happily boomed out the tune that *was* in the book. The vicar conducted at a brisk breakneck tempo with which it was possible to keep pace provided you didn't have to breathe. And judging by the purple faces at the conclusion of the hymn most of the congregation managed it.

During the singing of the psalms the choir had things their own way. Obviously the pointing was a deep mystery to the vicar, and he was sensible enough to let the choir flounder through in the old way rather than attempt to introduce a new way of floundering. The psalm, however, was a long one, and I suppose he considered we'd had more than our share of the limelight because when the time for the anthem arrived he said that as the congregation were in such good voice would they like to have a go at another hymn rather than listen to others singing. So as soon as the organist had found the place, and said some things one should never say in the presence of a church organ, we all roared forth again.

Then came the big attraction. The vicar announced that in place of his advertised sermon – it had been advertised in letters of scarlet and midnight blue on the noticeboard and below the amusements column in the local press – a great friend of his would now give a really intriguing talk, illustrated by colour transparencies, of course, on Old Church Organs. His friend happened to be in the neighbourhood and the opportunity seemed too good to miss. He'd travelled all over the place and knew all about Old Church Organs.

My friend whispered to me that the choir also knew all about Old Church Organs. Their organ was so old it was falling to bits. It had been second-hand when the church was built, and the church council hadn't spent a penny on it for donkey's years.

At the bottom of the church a man began setting up a projector, and two others pinned a large white sheet on the chancel screen. Vaguely realizing that the choir were now completely cut off the vicar suggested that they might like to learn something, if would they come down into the nave. Or they could go home quietly. We all went home quietly. Only the organist stayed behind. A PCC meeting was in the offing and he wanted to see the secretary to make sure that the question of the blowing motor was on the agenda. For years he had made sure the question of the blowing motor was on the agenda . . .

23

A Cunning Plan

In the village church where I recently inflicted myself on the choir, the organ was under repair, and the whole place was in a state of fantastic chaos. The story behind the affair was interesting, and strikingly illustrated the deep intelligence of lady vicars and parochial church councils.

Fearing that the organist would either resign or accomplish a complete mental breakdown unless they at last heeded his ten years of pleading, bullying and threatening, the church council issued an appeal for the repair fund. But it met with little initial success. Tastefully roped to the medieval porch, an outsized Essexboard thermometer, designed to show a rapid progress to the £100,000 target, remained for months showing no sign of raising above the £201.50 mark. Despite warnings of an imminent breakdown the organ still managed to drown the choir each Sunday, and naturally the congregation merely thought that the organist was being even more awkward than usual.

So the church council, shamelessly, with the backing of the vicar's brilliant feminine intuition, decided upon a plan of incredible cunning. Quietly they put the work to hand, and saw to it that the dismantled organ was spread generously all over everyone's favourite isolated pew. This meant that members of the congregation had no alternative but to sit within a few feet of each other in the same aisle – a most uncivilized practice much frowned upon in parts of the Church of England. And for good measure the organist arranged for the veteran vestry piano to deputize for the organ. It was this that broke the spirits of the congregation. Even those stalwarts who bravely managed to endure the ordeal of sitting together were beaten by the piano. No normal beings, apart from the choir (and there is always some doubt about choirs being normal), could survive this fiendish instrument for long.

In no time at all the entire £100,000 had been eagerly subscribed, and the vicar, in a prepared statement, said how deeply moved she was by the generous and spontaneous response . . .

On the Sunday evening I applied for temporary membership of the choir, the organist said he would be delighted to have me if I thought I could sing with the bad-tempered piano. I was able to set his mind completely at rest on this point. I explained that as a boy I had been trained under a distinguished choirmaster who had charmed great music out of a piano that had spent the best years of its life on a Thames pleasure launch. He had never achieved the impossible and charmed great music out of me, but at least he had taught me how to disguise the natural paper-and-comb quality of my voice.

As we reached the vestry, three or four choirboys

were manhandling the piano into the chancel. It was mounted on a trolley with little iron wheels that were not high enough to prevent one of its broken castors from gouging an intermittent rut in the vestry floor. And where the castor failed, the little iron wheels succeeded. The vicar called out encouragingly, 'Jolly good, splendid, boys,' and asked them to be just a little bit careful not to collide with a pile of new organ pipes that had appeared just inside the chancel door. Her appeal was either too late or just went unheeded, because for minutes afterwards it seemed we couldn't hear ourselves speak for the curious sound of rolling organ pipes on tessellated tiles.

Then, as everyone began to relax again, a Very Important Churchwarden sailed into the vestry and made the suggestion that the choir should sing unaccompanied for this service, as his wife's sister was in the congregation. She was on holiday from Wimbledon where she attended a very musical church, and he wanted her to leave with a reasonable impression of the singing and without a shattered nervous system. But the vicar was firmly in favour of the piano. In her gratitude she wanted the congregation to realize just how important their response to the organ appeal had been. And after all, she wasn't really interested in the opinion of the people who dropped in from musical churches in Wimbledon. So the Very Important Churchwarden, deflated, retired and we all trooped into the choir stalls.

A glance down the nave showed me that although we were starting a good ten minutes late, the majority of the congregation were still ambling in. The vicar tapped her feet, and waited in the manner of a conductor at the opera who holds up the overture while the usual moronic latecomers trample over everyone's feet to their seats. But the vicar didn't quite command the attention of a conductor. It was only when we commenced the first hymn, with the tin-can support of the piano, that people realized that proceedings were under way. They moved smartly to their places, dropped a number of coins, and walking sticks, and tidily folded their raincoats and patted them into the corners of their pews. By the time we had reached the last verse nearly all of them had opened their hymn books. Throughout the service the piano fulfilled its purpose magnificently. Minute by minute, those who had raised the money to reinstate the organ so quickly must have felt more and more grateful to themselves.

As we sat for the sermon the whole church was plunged into a coal-cellar-like gloom, with only a single lighted bulb dramatically displaying the vicar and the dry rot in the fine Jacobean pulpit. I have sometimes wondered at the widespread popularity of the practice of dousing the lights for the sermon. I understand on good authority that the reasons are to enable those who so desire to concentrate on the preacher, to save electricity, and to allow the bulk of the congregation to enjoy an unobtrusive nap. But no one slept on this occasion. The vicar dropped her bombshell before they could even settle down. In a brief address she explained that in addition to the agreed repairs to the organ, it had now been found necessary to fit a new blower-motor. (This is the modern counterpart of the boy who used to pump the bellows, the difference being that whereas the boy sometimes failed on duty and had to be started by a sharp cuff, the motor just breaks down and can't be started at all.)

The vicar explained eagerly that the sooner the additional cost could be met – and she knew the congregation would again respond generously – the sooner they could dispense with the piano. She turned to regard the organist already poised over the keyboard. With scarce concealed glee she announced the last hymn.

24

Dressed for Church

The choir at a favourite church of mine are renowned far and wide for being immaculately turned out, with stylish cassocks and gowns and ever crisp gleaming surplices, all supported by shining black shoes. They haven't always presented this pristine appearance. The transformation came some years ago (before ladies graced the choir, let it be said), when a father of a bride strongly objected to his fairy-tale bedecked daughter being preceded up the aisle by – as he complained to the vicar after the ceremony – 'a bunch of characters who looked as though they'd been outfitted from a discarded clothes stall and had just got the worst of it in a pub brawl'. And he had added that their singing was 'like you might hear from the same pub late on a Saturday night after a rugby final'.

The then vicar had taken immediate, firm action and from that time the choir had unfailingly presented their now famed vision of dress perfection at every service. True, in the matter of singing the organist, unlike the vicar, had not taken immediate firm action, or indeed any sort of action at all – he never liked to upset the choir – and there are some members of the congregation who reckon that the bride's father's description of the choir's singing remains very true today.

But the choir are not at all worried about these critics. Thanks to the recent addition of girls into this hitherto all-male organization their numbers are considerably increased and now almost everyone in the congregation has a connection with someone in the choir. And as the latest vicar keeps on drumming into everyone that they are all part of one great happy, helping family (the previous vicar who had transformed the choir's appearance would never have dreamed of suggesting such a sensational thing), and likes putting on services where you have to keep on shaking hands and hugging each other, it's a bit difficult for anyone to have a go at the choir and still appear happy and helpful.

On a recent warm summer Sunday morning the choir processed into church impressively immaculate, to sing choral matins. I was with them on one of my all-too-rare visits, looking forward to a pleasant hour singing my favourite hymns and chanting my favourite chants and listening to my favourite sermon. The vicar always preaches basically the same sermon, with only surface variations to suit the immediate circumstances. It is a highly entertaining diversion about his experiences as a plumber in the days before his wife got him interested in becoming a priest, thus dispensing with the necessity of having a disreputable van parked on the path across the front door and the task of dealing with an endless flow of unwashable washing.

We moved into the choir stalls with dignified precision and made a splendid colourful picture of uniformity. The organist was quite out of the picture behind a smart blue velvet curtain, so no one minded that he had not yet got round to wearing his new cassock and surplice and effected still his original dress of shirt sleeves in summer and darned pullover and scruffy neck scarf in winter. And to tell the truth, his mode of dress seems far more in sympathy with the spirit of the family service (which precedes matins at this church) than the faultless formality of the choir's attire.

Among the family service congregation the idea seems to be to outdo each other in informal garb. There are the usual jeans, both the vaguely presentable and the types that look as though they'd fall to bits if you washed them. There are the summer shorts whose colours put Jacob's coat to shame, and footwear that is to say the least startling and in some cases on a hot summer morning non-existent. One of two middle-aged gentlemen who take up the collection generally wears a yellow and red T-shirt emblazoned with the word SMILE and the other sports an off-white affair recommending someone's beer. On the other hand the matins congregation all wear well-cut suits and blazers or discreetly expensive dresses and footwear. They don't all huddle together like the family service supporters but sit about the church in their own little islands looking quietly assured and rather elegant.

The choir like matins more than the family service because at matins they sing music they never have to practise because they've sung it regularly for years, long before the introduction of the family service with its new hymns (firmly called 'praise songs' by the vicar) and its special 'turns' and surprise items slipped in here and there so that people won't become bored. To be fair, though, the family service praise songs don't really need practising either because you only have to beat time by clapping or stamping and look as though you are enjoying it all and they sing themselves.

And let it be said, the vicar infinitely prefers the family service where the praise songs are regularly bawled. In common with many vicars today he equates informality and vacuous verse and music with sincerity of worship and true Christian fellowship. Well-meaning fellow that he undoubtedly is, however, he does play his part at matins when he can't get anybody else to conduct it and always gives members of the matins congregation a cheery smile when he thinks he recognizes any of them in the street.

At this particular matins service the choir were indulging themselves with a particularly florid Victorian setting of the Te Deum which disturbed the vicar not a little because there seemed no way you could accompany it by clapping or doing a merry jig. But as always he put on a brave face and grinned encouragingly at some small girl recruits in the choir who were coping with vintage Stainer very well, having first removed their chewing gum and stuck it in the usual place under the book-rest. And so matins rolled comfortably on its splendid formal way. I enjoyed spotting the subtle alterations to suit the situation that the vicar made in his 'When I was a plumber' sermon and we finished strongly with 'Oh happy band of pilgrims', which we found most invigorating as the organist set such a fast pace on the organ that the pilgrims ended up not merely 'onward treading' but positively bounding.

In the vestry after the service we carefully hung up our gorgeous robes in the appointed place, the vicar in a spirit of true Christian charity thanked us for singing so beautifully such beautiful music, and the organist, he of the shirt sleeves and no sense of decorum, emerged from the organ loft and called out, 'Talk about *hot* up there! Anyone for a pint? My treat.' Two or three of the choirmen thought this a good idea and moved off smartly with the organist. An explosive rearguard of choirboys and girls followed and I was left alone in the vestry fiddling with my camera, with which I planned to take some photographs of the interior of the belfry.

Presently the vicar, who had been shaking hands vigorously, indeed violently some called it, with the tail-end of the matins congregation who had not been quick enough to escape, whirled back through the vestry. As he whirled he shouted how grand it was to see me in the choir again and what a pity I'd missed the family service, as it was particularly jolly this morning. They had a visiting priest, a simply *great* colleague who did some really amazing magic for the children, and one of the children's fathers who was a weightlifter had given a demonstration.

'Do I look stupid?'

I turned, startled, to be confronted by a large, fuming contralto choirlady to whom everyone in the choir showed proper respect at all times and tried to avoid at all costs, particularly when she cornered you and demanded to know if she looked stupid. This was always a prelude to the lady telling you of her latest collision with the vicar, the organist or the entire church council, about the shenanigans they got up to at the family service, and expecting your unquestioning support in making the vicar, organist and church council feel thoroughly guilty and unconditionally repentant.

'Do I look stupid?' the lady repeated.

I'd never really thought about it. I assured her quickly that I didn't think she looked stupid, and this seemed to make her even more cross.

'Just *listen*,' she commanded. 'I've been insulted – the whole choir have been insulted.'

'Ah,' I managed.

'It's that *man*,' she said.

'The vicar's warden?' I hazarded.

'Of course,' she hooted – she's that kind of contralto. 'He's just spoken to me. He actually expects me to *believe* that the only reason the choir won't be wanted at his daughter's wedding service at Christmas is because there's a choral society at her firm that she conducts and she wants *them* to sing the special music she's chosen. He says that the decision in no way reflects unfavourably on the beauty of *our* singing that gives him so much joy at matins every Sunday – balderdash!'

'He does tend to exaggerate,' I agreed.

'Exaggerate!' she roared. 'At the choir dinner last year he said that fine attire couldn't disguise mediocrity.'

'Perhaps he was referring to the bishop,' I said. 'He was the guest of honour, wasn't he?'

She glared at me. She tried again. 'He doesn't *like* the

choir,' she stated simply, her tone suddenly gentle and kindly as of one trying to enlighten a particularly dense infant.

'He doesn't like *anybody*,' I said. 'He can't stand the family service lot.'

A quite unexpected silence followed my words. The lady, with another change of tone, mumbled meditatively, 'True, true. Come to think of it I've often heard him tearing them to bits. Yes, I suppose he's not so bad really.'

From a row of fading sepia photographs on the wall above our magnificent choir robes half a dozen Victorian vicars gazed down at us. I wondered what they were thinking.